MW00448190

Cosmic Laws

by

Nada-Yolanda

Researched and Compiled by Douglas Earl Grant

MARK-AGE
Pioneer, Tennessee, USA

Revision of Mark-Age periodicals
of same title published 1996–1997.

© 2004, 1997, 1996 by Mark-Age, Inc.
All rights reserved.

Cover design by Christa Couture.

Bible quotations:
George M. Lamsa translation and New International Version

This book, or parts thereof, may not be reproduced
in any form without the prior written consent of:
Mark-Age, Inc.
P.O. Box 10
Pioneer, Tennessee 37847, USA

E-mail: iamnation@aol.com
Website: http://www.thenewearth.org/markage.html

ISBN-10: 0-912322-60-8
ISBN-13: 978-0-912322-60-5
Library of Congress Control Number: 2004107839

FIRST EDITION—2004
SECOND EDITION—2008

Manufactured in the United States of America
by Offset Paperback Mfrs., Inc., Wilkes-Barre, Pennsylvania

CONTENTS

Cosmic Laws

PREFACE

Alone on top of Mount Sinai, Moses had one of the great cosmic revelations of all time: he received the Ten Commandments. I wish I could say the same. But such was not the case when I authorized Douglas Earl Grant to collect cosmic laws from the vast amount of channeled communications of ascended masters through me since 1958.

In 1960, I had joined with El Morya-Mark (Charles B. Gentzel) to establish Mark-Age, Inc., in Miami, Florida. After his death in 1981, I continued to be executive director for life, training longtime Mark-Age members to become the staff of experts.

In 1983, Douglas Earl Grant and I had worked out an outline of subjects to be covered in the Geophysics School of the University of Life division of Mark-Age. The subjects dealt with spiritualizing man's relationship with nature–the plant, animal and mineral kingdoms. The central question was: by what means can living beings relate to one another justly and with spiritual consistency? Are there divine rules of life that govern human relationships with animals, plants and minerals? Are these principles so universal that they apply to animal–plant relationships, and plant–mineral relationships as well?

If so, these universal or cosmic laws would have to extend to relationships between life forms of Earth and those of other planes, planets and dimensions, including visitors from other planets. The more I thought about it, the more I became convinced that there had to be a set of divine principles that applied to every individual, no matter where or in what kingdom, that elucidated how to correctly, lovingly relate with one another.

In this book we will describe a partial listing, if not a complete one, of spiritual truths so universal that they can be considered cosmic laws. Truths of this stature, once learned, improve not only this life but all future incarnations. This applies whether we reside on this planet or another, in the astral planes or on the etheric planes, from now to eternity, no matter what the situation or the type of life form we are in relationship with. Cosmic laws are the most basic, fundamental ideas of Divine Mind, the principles through which all have their existence and are sustained. Biblically speaking, they comprise God's will. By comprehending these laws we can know God's will.

These are laws of God: oneness, individuality, polarity, love, creation, integration, transmutation, sacrifice, equality, give-and-take, free will, noninterference, order, cause and effect, reincarnation, growth and evolution, attraction and repulsion, righteousness, example, balance and harmony, compensation, life, perfection.

Created by God as spiritual beings, we already know these laws. We have lived in consonance with them before our present life, and will do so again in future lives. For they are the normal standards for living in the higher realms throughout Spirit's universe. In truth, as we study, meditate on and incorporate these principles into our daily lives, we are only remembering what we already know.

Throughout history, humankind has been driven, compelled, to discover what is behind existence. What is its purpose? What caused life? How? Why? Proof of the timelessness of cosmic laws, and of our quest of them, can be found in the writings or sayings attributed to the great teachers, prophets, philosophers and scientists of the ages. The universal laws and guidelines given by the masters of the spiritual Hierarchy in these modern times, which provide the basis for this book, are the same as those given to other civilizations down through the millennia.

For example, in a channeling through me on May 17, 1972, Sananda, Prince or spiritual ruler of Earth whose last incarnation was as Christ Jesus of Nazareth, revealed how we may discern whether our actions are based on truth and law: "Can you apply the same to the animal, the vegetable, the mineral kingdoms and the planet itself in order to make this demonstration?" The demonstration Sananda refers to is attaining spiritual consciousness and anchoring our I Am, light body.

Twenty-four hundred years ago, Socrates, another incarnation of Sananda, was in a Greek jail waiting to be put to death. Nevertheless, as Plato records in *Phaedo,* he was engaged in a remarkable discussion about reincarnation with another philosopher, Cebes, who was unconvinced of the truth of reincarnation. Socrates conveyed this point to his contemporary: "Do not regard the question only as it affects human beings, if you want to understand it readily, but also as it applies to all animals and plants, and, in fact, to everything that is 'born.' "

This book brings together modern channeled communications of divine principles, through my instrumentation, with guidance that ascended masters in former Earth incarnations, and other enlightened people, taught and wrote.

As we shall discover through the course of this study, the consistent transmission of divine truth, laws and knowledge from age to age is very comforting. It is written in the *Tao te ching,* a compilation of the teachings of Lao Tzu, the founder of Taoism (and an incarnation of the master Kut Humi): "Let your wheels move only along old ruts." If we wish to remain "comfortable" and stay in a rut, then why not let our habits conform to the oldest and deepest ruts of all, the eternal laws of God?

Oneness. Individuality. Polarity. Love. Creation. Integration. Transmutation. Sacrifice. Equality. Give-and-Take. Free Will. Noninterference. Order. Cause and Effect. Reincarnation. Growth and Evolution. Attraction and Repulsion. Righteousness. Example. Balance and Harmony. Compensation. Life. Perfection. Let us familiarize ourselves with these principles. They will never become obsolete.

Some of us have known of these laws, or some of them, and have lived in agreement with them for a long time; for others, they may be very new concepts, when viewed as divine laws. Either way, begin to put these laws into practice to see what good fruits they will bear. Pray and visualize that all on Earth do the same.

3

For the moment, at least, set aside the candles, put the cards back in the box, shelve the crystals and wands, forgo numbers, and place the charts back in the drawer. Take time out from rote prayers, mantras, rituals, ceremonies, visualizations, chanting and drumming. Strip naked mentally and emotionally to the depths of your soul, as Moses did, and face God. Have a talk. Receive personal inspirations about cosmic laws. And, like Moses, write them down.

May God bless us all, each and every one.

Love in action,

Nada - Yolanda

I Am Nation
Pioneer, Tennessee

INTRODUCTION

GOD'S WILL

When in doubt, ask that God's will be done. But how do we recognize that divine guidance so that we may follow it? To know cosmic laws is to discover what God's will is and how God operates. Cosmic laws describe the divine variables Spirit would have us consider before making a decision. In a manner of speaking, they tell us what Spirit would do if Spirit were in our place. The reality is that we are inseparable from the Divine; consequently, Its immutable laws continually animate the divine presence within each of us.

This relationship between man, God and divine law is set forth by Sananda in a communication on August 18, 1970: "Let us now grasp a few concepts and make them steadfast in our eternal determination to give righteous and loving proof of the fundamental laws within this universe from which we are created and out of which we have our sustenance and existence. . . . In the beginning was the Divine Creator. Before this there was always the Divine Creator, or Principle Itself. So there never was a time, never can be a time, when this is not the fundamental reasoning and thought power."

In this same discourse, Sananda states: "God is law. God is all the attributes and divine principles that exist throughout all creations. God is not an individualized soul or personal aspect of being, but that One which is all that can be, all that ever has been and all that ever shall be, and exists in all forms of creation. Those who come to this consciousness, those who have this concept, those who can enact these principles and teach them and demonstrate them are as gods, or Godlike."

For anyone who was brought up in a traditional religion where God or an aspect of God is thought of as a personal divine being, who speaks and has other characteristics much like a human being, this may seem a very radical idea. But the One God understood as Principle Itself is extremely important to our spiritual development. For it is through divine principles that we see with our minds the immaterial image and likeness of God.

It is written in Genesis 1:26 of the Torah: "And God said, 'Let us make man in our image, after our likeness.'" It is interesting that the singular One God of Judaism, which is history's preeminent bastion of monotheism, said let *us* make man after *our* image and likeness. This is known as a majestic plural. The Hebrew term, *Elohim,* is the plural form of one word used for God or Divinity. It is the most frequently used word for Divinity in the Torah.

Majestic plurals can be found in many religious teachings where man sincerely is trying to comprehend God and learn how to be like God; for example, the Father–Son–Holy Spirit trinity in Christianity, the Elohim of Judaism, and the Brahma–Vishnu–Shiva trinity of Hinduism. The divine laws that make up the Lord God, which means laws of God, of the Bible are embodied as different gods in some religions and different aspects of the One God in others.

The problem is that in religious practices on every continent of this world for thousands of years many of the gods, goddesses and deities do not accurately personify the divine principles ascribed to them. Moreover, many of the laws or principles of science and philosophy do not fully conform to spiritual laws either.

All of the changes that are occurring now in man's consciousness and manifesting in the outer world can be traced back to the misunderstanding and misapplication of Spirit's laws, which is to say, Principle Itself. As for humanity in the Latter Days, the day of judgment, an Old Testament psalmist proclaimed: "They know not, neither will they understand; they walk on in darkness; all the foundations of the earth are shaken."

On Thanksgiving Day, 1986, in my Nada Self, I channeled a similar pronouncement for the Hierarchy: "The day of judgment has arrived. . . . Man is about to reap the consequences of his unbalanced behavior in every aspect of life as we know it. It will seem as though all foundations upon which he lives and acts and has his being in this environment are going to be removed."

In a channeling on September 1, 1968, Lord Michael, the angelic head of the spiritual Hierarchy, explained what people's reactions will be as they make the transition to the higher standard of cosmic laws in these Latter Days:

"I am here speaking of a higher law, of a higher understanding, of a higher examination that is revealed in the spiritual consciousness of man rather than in his own intellectual prowess, where he has set up the laws and the rules of truth and is not concerned with what has been set down for him to take unto himself. In this way he is in for more shocks and more deprivations and greater upsets of his faculties and grounding in Earth than in any other department, for he has created religions and laws and methods of communication which are not satisfactory to the laws of divine truth."

Along these same lines, Sananda relayed additional guidance on July 19, 1967: "Could man only understand and evolve his consciousness to the point where he realizes all physical law is under the spiritual, divine guidance and purpose, and can be changed if and when it serves a higher purpose and law. Now that the higher purpose and law are about to become manifested upon the Earth, naturally some of these physical laws will not be applicable, or will seem to change, and thereby upset all standards, rules, measurements which man has attributed to them.

"You are about to see this confusion, because what has been calculated or figured, according to man's physical understanding and his mental acclimatization, shall become null and void by something superseding it. That something will be the truer, higher, fundamental control of Spirit in action upon the Earth."

When Archangel Michael states that man's greatest deprivations, upsets and shocks will be because of man-made laws, wisdom dictates that we reevaluate the foundation upon which we stand: our values and religious beliefs, our reliance on others, and our goals in life during these Latter Days before the Second Coming. In what do we have faith? Are we putting our faith in anything other than Spirit

Itself? If we are, we and our faith will be shaken—not by God but by us. Spirit and Its laws are unshakable, immutable, eternal, transcendent and perfect. The fault will be ours for believing in ideas that are partially or completely untrue and for relying on people or institutions that incorporate ill-conceived or erroneous ideas.

For example, at one end of the spectrum are those who pray for and rely solely on the Messiah, Sananda-Jesus the Christ of Nazareth, personally to save them. It is true that he will return in this new millennium to exemplify the methods and forces that are the products of divine laws which govern both physical and spiritual energy frequencies, the third and the fourth dimension, respectively. But as one individual child of God, he personally is not our savior.

At the other end of the spectrum are many who think that visitors from other planets will save them in these end days. This, too, misses the whole purpose of Spirit's plan and program for Earthman's spiritual evolvement. What the space visitors and Sananda-Jesus bring to man are teachings of the higher, fundamental laws of God. Unfortunately, this upsets terribly the scientific community and all areas of society, business, religion and education, wherever science and religion have set the foundation of our modern civilization on imperfect standards, rules, measurements and concepts.

God alone saves us. In other words, our salvation comes from utilizing spiritual principles in every department of life. By following the will of God and loving one another, we are freed from sin or error.

One of China's foremost philosophers, Mo Tzu, lived in the fifth century before Christ. He instructed the people of his day in these same concepts:

"The will of Heaven to me is like the compasses to the wheelwright and the square to the carpenter. The wheelwright and the carpenter apply their square and compasses to measure all square and circular objects in the world. They say that those that fit are correct and those that do not fit are not correct. The writings of the scholars and gentlemen of the world today cannot all be loaded in carts and the many doctrines they teach cannot all be enumerated. They try to persuade the feudal lords above and various minor officials below. But as to humanity and righteousness, they are far, far off the mark. How do I know? I say: I have the shining model in the world (the will of Heaven) to measure them."

In the twenty-three cosmic laws presented in this book we have the shining model that is the will of God. So, whenever we have our doubts, which we no doubt will have between now and the Second Coming, let us ask that God's will be done. It is among the most powerful thoughts a child of God can think.

ONENESS

God is One. God is coherent. Through His perfect unity and co-herence, God becomes comprehensible. The first truth we realize from God's oneness is that we are united unconditionally and eter-nally with Spirit. Once we grasp this reality, a second truth emerges: complete separation from God is utterly impossible.

We begin our study with the law of oneness because God's one-ness makes God coherent. *Coherent* has a twofold meaning here. God is coherent because all that God is, is integrated as one. Nothing exists outside of Spirit's presence. And because of Spirit's unity, God becomes intelligible (that is, coherent) to mankind and, to one degree or another, all other life forms created by Spirit.

Let us examine two broad categories of man's quest in compre-hending oneness. We are all aware of the tremendous discoveries in physics about how God's energy and matter are unified. Albert Einstein (1879–1955) is credited as being a genius in large part for his achievement in mathematically describing the integrity of energy and matter on a large scale. With elegant simplicity he described his theory of relativity by the now-famous equation, $E = mc^2$.

For the remainder of his beautiful life, Einstein continued his quest to combine small-scale energies and particles to larger ones in a unified set of equations, the Unified Field Theory. He often felt a sense of awe during this pursuit, and he once wrote, "The most incomprehensible thing in the universe is that it is comprehensible."

Likewise, in the biological sciences a deepening awareness of the interconnectedness of life has created new discoveries and even whole new fields of science, such as ecology. As a result, scientists of widely diverse interests have become interdisciplinary. For example, international conferences on the environment, AIDS, ecology, ozone and the greenhouse effect have brought together scientists of many disciplines the world over to work on global problems which affect all planetary life. Truly, humanity is beginning to uncover the total interdependence of God's creation.

If this is true in the study of God's physical universe, how much more so must it be true for us, spiritual scientists if you will, in our metaphysical quest to understand God's oneness.

Some of the greatest spiritual scientists have come from the Hasidic branch of Judaism. In the eighteenth century, the founder of Hasidism, Israel Baal Shem Tov, spoke of the unity of God and His commandments.

As Rabbi Aryeh Kaplan relates in *The Light Beyond: Adventures in Hassidic Thought,* "The Baal Shem Tov said in the name of the earlier masters that one should realize the mystery of God's unity. Whenever we grasp hold of any part of this unity, we grasp it all. . . .

"The Torah and Commandments emanate from God's Essence, which is true Unity. Therefore, when you observe even a single commandment correctly with love and attachment, you grasp part of the Unity through this commandment.

"All of this Unity is then in your hands. Since all the commandments are included in this Unity, it is then as if you kept them all."

Here, then, is one of the most important keys we will ever learn about God's oneness and magnificence. God's laws are integrated, not disintegrated. Therefore, the definition of any one of the divine laws must include all other universal principles.

Take love, for example. By knowing that divine love includes all other divine laws, we better understand how to express love correctly. Divine love requires us to know our oneness with God and with one another, and to realize that every act of love causes a positive effect. Love also will cause transmutation or change to occur in our lives. Love requires us to give and take, to be orderly, and to make sacrifices. True love brings our unique individuality into expression and safeguards our free will so that it will be in balance and harmony with others. Love assures the continuance of our individual and collective spiritual growth and evolvement.

Add the rest of God's laws to this list and a clear vision emerges: only through the manifestation of all spiritual principles can one law truly be brought to life.

On October 26, 1971, Archangel Chamuel channeled additional information on the oneness of God's nature: "It is only in Divine Mind that we can even subdivide the one, the whole, the all, which is God, to begin with. So, if we look at the mathematical formulas we see that the one unified God, which is all that there is, is indivisible. Yet, within that indivisibility there are . . . aspects that can be conceived of by reasoning, intellectual, and even spiritual, mind consciousness. . . .

"When you pick up a solid form and see it as a whole, you still can see two sides of it. Yet, it is not divided in itself, it is whole. Such is the nature of God energy, life force, light and creation. All of creation together is one, as part of the One; and undivided in this respect, for God sees no division in Himself or in His creations."

As we live and breathe, let these words be foremost in our thoughts and in our hearts. We experience divine oneness as God intends by seeing no division in ourselves, between ourselves and Spirit, and between ourselves and every other living being. By these actions are we raised, mathematically speaking, to the power of One.

The change that will occur in us and in humankind will be this: the irreversible decrystallization of the curse that makes us think that we can be separate from our Creator. Jesus addressed this very subject in a communication on October 18, 1960:

"We continue to think of ourselves as separate from the Christ within, as though we can have an existence away from, in spite of, or

11

in addition to the Spirit that is within us equally. This is man's original sin, and no other. There is no separation, there can be no separation. The hell and the torment and the sins that follow from this original sin are the sins created upon sin from thinking we are separate from God. God has created us, each of us, and God stands with us whether we stand with God or not. . . .

"I am most serious upon this communication in relaying this most basic and profound thought. It is the essence of all my teachings for every incarnation I ever have lived upon the face of this globe, or on any other dimension or other planet that I have taken up a sojourn. This is the essence of all religion, of all philosophy, of all being. Recognize that you are the creation of the Holy Spirit within and depend upon that Spirit to guide you, to teach you and to bring you into the full glory of God awareness, or Christ consciousness."

Jesus' powerful example of being one with God and of seeing no separation at all is our guiding light. In that lifetime, he stilled storms, raised the dead, healed every kind of disease, manifested food for thousands of people, and performed many other miracles. He possessed fantastic powers, a tremendous ability to manipulate energy. But according to the Gospel of John, what did he say over and over again in various ways? "I can do nothing of myself. I do not seek my will." Why? He and the Father, God, were one. Not two. One.

In that oneness, Jesus knew that the Lord God, the laws of God, perform all actions. He alone and we alone can do nothing by ourselves. To know this is to comprehend oneness, and to experience true humility.

As we dwell on our oneness with God and all of God's creations, let us absorb one more example of Jesus' profound demonstration of being one with Spirit. But first, review how many pressures, problems and responsibilities we each have in our lives: family, business, personal, spiritual and so forth. Now think about the responsibilities Jesus had in his incarnation: to himself, to his disciples, to his family, to all the souls on Earth at that time and for thousands of years hence, amounting to billions of human incarnations. This was his burden as the Christ exemplar for mankind.

He said, "Come to me, all you who labor and carry burdens, and I will give you rest. Take my yoke upon you, and learn from me, for I am gentle and meek in my heart, and you will find rest for your souls. For my yoke is pleasant and my burden is light."

Can it be even conceivable that his burden was, and still is, light? He knew full well the crushing weight of his responsibility to every life form on this planet as its spiritual way shower. And yet he said his burden was light. He must have been out of his mind! Yes. He was definitely out of his mind in that he was not speaking from mortal consciousness. Those were the words of one in I Am consciousness, whose union with God is total.

If his tremendous burden was light, what is this yoke that is pleasant? What is it that one can shoulder to make the heavy burdens of life light? It can be none other than the laws of God. Jesus said that the greatest of these is love. What, then, is love divine? All of the laws of God manifesting through us in unison to perfection.

Our Heavenly Father, Holy/Wholeness is Your Name.

Shema Yisrael, Adonoy Elohenu, Adonoy Echad. "Hear, O Israel [all children of God]: the Lord our God, the Lord is One."

INDIVIDUALITY

God's greatness is absolutely astounding! What we have learned of Spirit's majesty thus far becomes astonishingly magnified when we more fully comprehend the cosmic law of individuality.

Our journey to understand God takes us into the unfathomable vastness of Spirit's creation. How could we possibly experience anything as great as the law of oneness? Easy. We are about to explore how each individual creation of God, from the largest to the most minute, is unique, special and beyond compare. The truth that Spirit never duplicates Itself or any of Its creations finds its origin in this universal principle.

Many of us probably have heard phrases that reveal the fundamental relationship between the divine laws of oneness and individuality—"unity in diversity," for example. The motto of Jamaica is "Out of many, one people." It describes the diverse cultural and racial mix of people of that island nation united as one.

The connection between the principles of oneness and individuality is also evident in one of the original definitions of individuality. Today, individuality is defined as the sum of characteristics or qualities that set one person or thing apart from others. But a former definition, unfortunately now considered archaic, defines individuality as indivisibility, inseparability, a single being undivided. That certainly describes spiritual reality from the cosmic perspective. We are unique individuals united as one to a singular Supreme Being from whom we cannot separate ourselves.

Because individuality is an eternal, universal law we do not have to strive to be unique. We each have been created unique. Nor can we ever lose our uniqueness. These realities are closely related to the fact that we need not strive to create our Christ Self and light body. Our I Am Self already fully exists, cannot be destroyed, is unique and eternal. Therefore, our sole effort is to reawaken to our inherent Christ consciousness and powers. According to the law of individuality, we need only *rediscover* our unique purpose and function as spiritual beings.

As with each cosmic law, our first order of business is to personalize or internalize Spirit's divine statute. By experiencing this law as fully as we possibly can, we facilitate the release to our conscious mind of information we need to know about ourselves and our soul mission; that is, what we are meant to do in this lifetime in order to express and to develop our unique individuality and to serve humanity.

Not only do we want to know and to experience this law for ourselves, but we also desire the same for every other living being on this planet. In every kingdom all need to know the truth about themselves. This includes their uniqueness and how they may best serve others through their special expression of love.

On June 30, 1962, John Mark channeled information about the individuality of other life forms within this solar system: "As no two glands or organs in your own body operate at the same frequency or rate of vibration, nor have the same function or purpose within your own body, so the other planets within your solar system that do express so-called physical life, as you know it, do not have the exact same function or purpose within the solar system, nor do they vibrate at the same rate of frequency.

"Therefore, when you are in communication or when you are in contact physically, psychically or mentally with any of the beings of other physical planets, you will learn and will come to recognize that they are not exactly as you are, nor do they function or think or express themselves or have the same desires as you upon the Earth planet."

The planets in this solar system and the inhabitants on the various frequency planes of those planets have unique purposes and functions. In his book *Cosmos,* Carl Sagan wrote that there are some hundred billion galaxies, each with an average of a hundred billion stars. And in all the galaxies, there are possibly as many planets as stars, ten billion trillion. When John Mark's description of varied life forms of other planets is considered alongside the astronomical calculations of Carl Sagan, Spirit's tremendous diversity of unique, individual creations begins to become evident. This is but a glimpse of the macrocosmic manifestation of the divine law of individuality.

Serapis Bey, Chohan or Director of the Fourth Ray for the spiritual government of this solar system, channeled on February 26, 1969, the microcosmic view of this law:

"A crystal is an atomic structure unique and special unto itself, and never two alike; as every cell in your body is unique and special unto itself. Although each cell has a specific purpose and plan, and each cell in each one's body there relates to certain areas of function, they are similar and work in a specific area of their particular function. But no two are ever exactly alike; for there is significant difference and personality within each creative atom, neutron and proton alike.

"What man has not been able to determine yet is that within that creative force which we are speaking of, the very smallest energy particle, it differentiates via a sound vibration. It is within that sound frequency that the individuality or personality is determined, according to the highest spheres of intunement and realization."

Think about that the next time you take your vitamin pill. My multiple vitamin and mineral supplement has fifty milligrams of calcium. I take one tablet a day. In that one tablet, I'm not just ingesting fifty milligrams of calcium; I'm putting into my body approximately 752 million trillion individual calcium atoms; all with their own unique God-given radiance and personality!

The immensity of God's universe and the vast numbers of unique individuals staggers the mind. Taxonomists and biologists have estimated that three to twenty million plant and animal species now live on the planet and even more have become extinct. Man, all 6.7 billion of us, comprise but one single species: *Homo sapiens.* In religious terms, we are of one single congregation as well: the only begotten Son of God, the indwelling Christ spirit.

If all other creations of Spirit are unique, is it even possible to conceive that each human being is not unique, with a special gift to give to the world? According to a channeled communication from my Nada Self on August 21, 1970, it is not possible:

"From out of that Son millions upon billions of souls or cells are created with individualized identities and functions. No two are alike, no two have experienced alike. Out of the millions upon billions of souls or Selves, which we call I Am identities within, are created many souls' experiences. Each I Am identity or individualization has had myriad types of expressions and soul episodes."

This communication goes on to explain how we as Christed beings relate to one another, sharing information, feelings and experiences in service to the whole. In the evolution of man on and about this planet, a problem arose that still exists: "Here is where the error of man has been and he has continued to fall into disrepute and disgrace; or to fall from perfect balance, which is the meaning of disgrace. He has desired his brother's or his fellow creature's experience or responsibility."

This, then, is where the law of individuality within us becomes adulterated. We envy another's advantages, possessions, superior knowledge, powers or wealth of any kind. Individually and as a race, we act in opposition to the law of individuality when we seize, occupy or enjoy the place, the power, the functions or the property of another without right. The Mosaic law is sharply clear on this point: "You shall not covet your neighbor's house, you shall not covet your neighbor's wife, nor his manservant, nor his maidservant, nor his ox, nor his ass, nor anything that is your neighbor's."

But the principle of individuality also relates to man's desire to place himself in and enjoy physical existence in a lower kingdom —the animal kingdom—rather than desiring his own creative functioning and responsibilities as a spiritual being on the etheric planes in I Am, light-body consciousness.

At the root of all greed, envy and lust for things outside of ourselves is the loss of the knowledge of our own uniqueness, identity and place in the universe; our own special purpose and contribution to the world, which God ingrained within us. We can only come to know our highest service by intunement with Spirit through our I Am Self.

The great diversity of life provides us with an opportunity to learn more about God than we ever could on our own, through sharing our different talents and experiences. We best serve one another and love God by cooperating and coordinating in this way. For none of us alone can be all or know all that is God.

Our eternal mandate is this: that we love the Lord our God and love one another by living out our unique Christ expression. That is all. That is enough. Our I am that I Am does not covet another's possessions. Our I am that I Am will not covet another's experience. Our I am that I Am cannot covet another's soul mission responsibilities.

This is all the more true now that the Second Coming is at hand.

In every kingdom, those on Earth and in its astral planes are incarnated at this special time in planetary history for a divine reason and with a divine contribution to make. So, let us affirm that we shall live the law of individuality and shall be satisfied in fulfilling our unique spiritual contribution, and thereby shall extinguish envy in all its many forms.

The Baal Shem Tov, founder of Hasidism, may have expressed it best when he said: "Every man should know that since creation no other man ever was like him. Had there been such another, there would be no need for him to be. Each is called on to perfect his unique qualities. And it is his failure to heed this call which delays the Messiah."

POLARITY

"Where two or more are gathered, there I Am. Thus you will learn and will experience and will demonstrate the basic, essential, fundamental, divine law of the two polarities, the conscious and the subconscious in one unified whole to bring about the I Am consciousness and the spiritual action in formation by materialization."

Our attention now turns to one of the most easily observable of cosmic laws: the law of polarity. Life and death, day and night, male and female, active and passive, macrocosmic and microcosmic: these are just a few of the many ways in which to view the principle of polarity. Even as children we perceived this divine law in the myriad opposites of our world. Polarity is the perfect example of how tangible all of God's laws truly are. All other universal laws are just as real, just as prevalent and just as powerful in our daily lives.

What could be more important for us than to discover a fundamental law like polarity that will help us to attain Christ consciousness? The quotation that opens this chapter was given by Sananda-Jesus, spiritual leader of Earth, on April 16, 1973. But we could just as easily go back to Sananda's own channelship as Moses at Mount Sinai over thirty-two hundred years ago to hear about the law of polarity. One of the ten laws he received from Spirit at that time was: Honor your father and your mother. Though the words are different, they pronounce the same law.

We each are created in the image of God, male and female. This is God's likeness. God is One who has a dual or polar nature: a father, or positive, masculine, active aspect and a mother, or negative, feminine, receptive aspect. Each human being, each life form, each manifestation is created likewise.

In channelings through me from the spiritual government of this solar system, God the Father is described as the positive pole. He is the idea to create, to be; the truth of light; the law of God, and positive energy. The Mother aspect, also referred to as the Holy Spirit or Holy Ghost, is the negative pole. She is that which formulates and brings forth the seed, or ideas emanating from the mind of God as thoughts and principles. She is light or enlightenment, Divine Mind, and negative energy.

From this description of the God Force, it can be seen that the terms *positive* and *negative* do not mean "good" and "evil." God is only good. Therefore, *positive* and *negative* describe two qualities of the one Divine Energy we call Spirit. God the Father is the Creator of law and God the Mother executes those laws.

Where do we as sons of God fit in? In a message on June 28, 1961, Dr. Hannibal-St. Germain of the spiritual Hierarchy explains: "In the Holy Trinity the Father represents the projector and the Mother is the receiver. These are the positive and negative poles. The Son represents the creation or the reaction of the two poles working equally, perfectly balanced and having the desired results. This is true in every realm. There is no realm or dimension known to us that does not operate on this simple procedure."

On Earth, however, humankind lives this simple procedure *imperfectly*. But with a true understanding of this divine law we can rediscover fundamental components of our I Am Self which, in turn, will revitalize our inherent spiritual consciousness, powers and talents.

Notice how the principle of polarity is reflected in the very names of some laws of God: cause and effect, give-and-take, attraction and repulsion. Though they are individual laws, their names express God's divine duality. Indeed, all cosmic principles have dual or polar aspects.

This also explains why many universal ideals seem so opposed to one another that one might think they were contradictory. Take, for example, the law of oneness and the law of individuality, the law of free will and the law of noninterference, or the law of sacrifice and the law of compensation. What can we understand from this? Neither individual cosmic laws nor their positive and negative aspects can be looked upon as conflicting qualities or forces in opposition to one another. Rather, they are complementary, cooperative aspects and ideas in harmony with one another. Their combination has an additive effect.

Therefore, we need not trouble ourselves with the question of which facet or pole of God's will as divine laws we should favor in any given circumstance. We must consider all equally in their interwoven totality.

A glance at nature will enable us to realize the goodness of balanced polarity. Male and female physical forms create a continuance of life in all kingdoms. Each atom of matter has a positive nucleus and a negatively-charged electron field around it. Water, the most important molecule on Earth for plant and animal life, is dipolar. Polarity-driven chemical reactions, from breathing to the formation of limestone in the oceans, uphold planetary life.

Electric and magnetic fields are created from positively-charged and negatively-charged bodies. When we perform an act as simple as turning on a light bulb, Spirit's principle of polarity is initiated. In the twentieth century, physicists discovered that light energy and matter both have a dual wavelike and particlelike nature. Whether man believes it or not, scientists already have proven God's existence by describing these and other expressions of the divine law of polarity in our universe.

As with every divine statute, Spirit gives us the free will to apply this law beneficially or detrimentally. One of the most spectacular cases of man's reprehensible manipulation of the polarity inherent in nature is the creation of the atomic bomb, which was conceived and designed to create a sustained *imbalance* of positive and negative energies within the atom.

The dangers of wrongfully employing cosmic law were not lost on the bomb's creators. The official press release of the United States War Department in 1945 described the first atomic bomb detonation this way: "The explosion came . . . pressing hard against the people and things, to be followed almost immediately by the strong sustained awesome roar which warned of doomsday and made us feel that we puny things were blasphemous to dare tamper with the forces reserved for the Almighty."

But this and similar problems related to the misuse of the law of polarity are dwarfed by the reason for these destructive activities: the unbalanced polarities of the human mind.

In relation to aspects of mind, the Hierarchy has described two standard ways of viewing divine polarity. One is that mortal consciousness is a functional duality of the conscious and the subconscious mind. The conscious, masculine, positive pole is our analytical, decision-making center through which we employ rational, logical means to compare information and weigh options before making choices and taking action. The feminine, negative aspect is the subconscious, the seat of our memory and feeling nature. Memories held in the subconscious act as a reservoir of information which can be tapped to promote understanding and facilitate choice. Also, spiritual inspirations and information are delivered via dreams and meditations from the superconscious through the subconscious to the conscious mind.

For us to do God's will, both the conscious and the subconscious mind must be equally respected and utilized. Disequilibrium of their functioning leads to different forms of imbalance. For example, the conscious aspect can override proper subconscious functioning through overbearing skepticism and sole dependence on the intellect. Overreliance on the conscious aspect can also tend to make us

21

regard dreams as irrelevant and meaningless, and thereby cut off a legitimate avenue through which we receive superconscious guidance from Spirit.

By the same token, a mind-set that favors subconscious activity to the exclusion of reasoned, conscious analysis can also lead to trouble; for instance, where inspirations, memory recall and information received in dream, meditation and intuition are exclusively depended upon and regarded as infallible. In such a situation, conscious discernment would be regarded as tampering with inner guidance that should be followed to the last detail. Hence, proper conscious functioning would be negated. Common sense would not be available, and this could result in the person living in a dreamworld that serves neither self nor anyone else.

The second way the Hierarchy describes the law of polarity in terms of mind is mortal and immortal consciousness. Jesus said, "Where two or three come together in my name, there am I with them." Metaphysically interpreted, when the two mortal aspects of consciousness—conscious and subconscious—are in balanced, equitable functioning, full integration with the superconscious, immortal aspect of consciousness is achieved. Thus, our mortal consciousness is translated into immortal, I Am, Christ consciousness.

So may each of us strive to restore the perfect balance of Spirit's divine polar expression within ourselves, which makes being one with our Father-Mother God possible through our superconscious, I Am Self.

As recorded in the Old Testament, Abraham, the father of Islam, Judaism and Christianity, heard the angel of the Lord call out: "Abraham! Abraham!" He replied: "Here am I."

Spiritually interpreted, the voice Abraham heard was that of Spirit by way of Its agents or his own superconscious Self. He "heard" his name twice, indicating he had received the divine contact of words and energies on both the subconscious and the conscious level. Because there were no blockages between the two polarities of his mortal mind, the mortal and immortal aspects of Abraham's consciousness were able to operate as an integrated whole. That he accomplished Spirit's will is a matter of historical record.

In a vision of the night, Jacob heard his name called: "Jacob, Jacob." He replied: "Here am I." In front of the burning bush, Moses heard the Living God call out: "Moses, Moses." He responded: "Here am I."

As with Abraham, both Jacob and Moses successfully received divine inspiration in both aspects of their mortal consciousness. They acknowledged the contact and union of their mortal and immortal aspects of consciousness by proclaiming: *Here I Am.*

An example of the effect of disequilibrium and negativity within the conscious and the subconscious mind is found in Paul's conversion, as recorded in Acts of the Apostles. On the road to Damascus, Saul (his name prior to conversion) was filled with anger and thoughts of murder against disciples of Jesus. As he neared the city, suddenly a light shone round about him and he fell to the ground. He heard the voice of the resurrected Christ Jesus say, "Saul, Saul, why do you persecute me?"

He responded: "Who are you, my Lord?" Because Saul held negative thoughts, he could not recognize with whom he was speaking. As an outer reflection of his clouded consciousness, he became blind, and remained so for three days until the Holy Spirit, through Ananias, healed him.

Unlike Saul, Samuel was pure in heart and mind. The Temple priest Eli taught him how to communicate with Spirit. As it is written in I Samuel, "The Lord came and stood there, calling as at the other times, 'Samuel! Samuel!' Then Samuel said, 'Speak, for Your servant is listening.' "

Invoking Spirit's help, we ask that each human being, according to his philosophy or faith, rediscover the law of polarity in the texts and scriptures upon which he bases his life.

Buddhists can realize the law of polarity through deep contemplation of the Middle Way, the way between extremes as Gautama himself taught it, and by discarding all lesser rituals and dogma. Taoists can experience this law most profoundly through comprehend-

23

ing the yin and the yang that is the Tao, the Way, which created all the seeming paradoxes of nature.

Zoroastrians can perceive the crucial role polarity plays in the divine law of free will by focusing on Zarathustra's teaching concerning the twin spirits created by Ahura Mazda, the "Lord of Light." One twin, Angra Mainyu, "the hostile spirit," represents the mortal, selfish use of free will. The other twin, Spenta Mainyu, "the benevolent spirit," represents immortal, selfless volition.

Confucianists can interpret polarity as a divine law in the classic texts *Great Learning* and *Doctrine of the Mean.* Likewise, followers of Judaism can enact ever more profoundly the commandment to honor the Father and the Mother God. Hindus can discover the relationship between the mortal self and the immortal Self, the polarity of "as above, so below," that is at the heart of the Upanishads and *Bhagavad Gita.*

Christians can satisfy the law of polarity by fulfilling Jesus' Sermon on the Mount teachings: love your enemies, bless those who curse you, do good to anyone who hates you, pray for those who persecute you. Through the power of positive thoughts, desires and actions, negativity is neutralized. Such is the law of polarity utilized to restore life's balance and harmony.

In the name of our Father-Mother God, we proclaim the authority of Spirit's law of polarity on and about this planet Earth, within each heart and within each mind. So, in each day of our lives and in each night that we sleep, all people will be able to say: "Lord, here am I. Here I Am. Speak, for Your servant is listening."

LOVE

Of all cosmic laws, the most universally known is love. Love as a spiritual principle has a rich, ancient and enduring presence in the history of religious ideas. In Africa during the civil wars that broke out after the Sixth Dynasty in Egypt, about 2200 B.C., one king composed a set of instructions for his son Meri-ka-Re: "Do justice whilst thou endurest upon Earth. . . . Do not do evil. . . . Love all men!"

In the thirteenth century B.C., during the wanderings in the wilderness by the Israelites returning from Egypt to the Promised Land, Moses composed guidelines for his people based on revelations from God: "You shall not hate your brother in your heart. . . . You shall not bear any enmity against the children of your own people, but you shall love your neighbor as yourself; I am the Lord. You shall keep My statutes."

Deep in the forests of the upper Ganges sometime in the first millennium B.C., an illumined master teacher set down thoughts for his disciples in what would become, centuries later, the *Bhagavad Gita:* "This supreme Lord who pervades all existence, the true Self of all creatures, may be realized through undivided love." As the mouthpiece of the Lord he writes: "I look upon all creatures equally; none are less dear to Me and none more dear. But those who worship Me with love live in Me, and I come to life in them."

Over two thousand years later, in modern India, a direct disciple of these teachings, Mahatma Gandhi, wrote: "It is my firm belief that it is love that sustains the earth. There only is life where there is love. Life without love is death."

In the fifth century B.C., when China's feudal system was disintegrating and war was on the horizon, a figure equal in rank to Confucius emerged, teaching a doctrine of universal love. Mo Tzu claimed: "Because of want of mutual love, all the calamities, usurpations, hatred, and animosity in the world have arisen. Therefore the man of humanity condemns it. . . . It should be replaced by the way of universal love and mutual benefit. . . . Those who love others will be loved by others. Those who benefit others will be benefited by others."

In the Middle East at the beginning of the common era, Jesus encouraged his disciples to love: "Just as my Father has loved me, I also have loved you; abide in my love. If you keep my commandments, you will abide in my love, even as I have kept my Father's commandments and abide in His love. . . . This is my commandment: That you love one another just as I have loved you."

The most famous divine law on Earth is also its greatest. One of the Pharisees who knew Mosaic law by heart asked Jesus, "Teacher, which is the greatest commandment in the law?" Jesus said to him: "Love the Lord your God with all your heart and with all your soul and with all your might and with all your mind. This is the greatest and the first commandment. And the second is like to it, Love your neighbor as yourself. On these two commandments hang the law and the prophets."

In a synopsis on love in *The Encyclopedia of Religion,* religious historian J. Bruce Long buttresses Jesus' assertion: "The concept of love, in one form or another, has informed the definition and development of almost every human culture in the history of the world—past and present, East and West, primitive and complex.

"Broadly conceived, love has been a motivational force in the shaping of culture within both the ideological and behavioral dimensions of life and a substantive theme in the by-products of almost every form of human activity: in religion and the arts, literature and music, dance and drama, philosophy and psychology. It is, perhaps, safe to say that the idea of love has left a wider and more indelible imprint upon the development of human culture in all its aspects than any other single notion."

People often say that they feel love. But how often do people claim that they understand love? If love is not understood, then who knows whether what they feel is love rather than something else, something less?

Love is currently defined as a strong affection for, or attachment or devotion to, a person or persons; a strong liking for or interest in something. Words most closely describing this type of friendly, loving feeling include the Greek *philia,* the Latin *delictio,* and *sneha* and *priyata* in Sanskrit.

Love also is depicted as a strong, usually passionate, affection for a person of the opposite sex. This type of love, which often is reduced to carnal desire for one's own pleasure and gratification, is encompassed by the words *eros* in Greek, *amor* in Latin and *kama* in Sanskrit.

Finally, the theological definition of love is divided into three aspects: (1) God's benevolent concern for mankind, (2) man's devout attachment to God, (3) the feeling of benevolence and brotherhood that people should have for one another.

The aforementioned words of Jesus on love certainly influenced this definition. However, apart from Christian influences, selfless divine love finds its expression in the Greek *agape,* the Latin *caritas,* the Sanskrit *karuna* used in Buddhism, the Sanskrit *prema* of Hinduism, the Arabic *rahman* and in Hebrew, *hesed.* Apart from other qualities of love, divine love was so distinctly recognized in civilizations, cultures and religions using these languages, that a specific term was required to describe it.

In the first definition of love, three key components emerge: affection, attachment and devotion. Fond or tender feelings of affection, a manifestation of love, can be witnessed in humanity and throughout nature in relationships involving parents and offspring. The bonding power of love is evinced by humanity's groupings: family, culture, tribe, society, nation and religion. Animals, plants and minerals that group into families, herds, flocks, communities and associations attest to the cohesive quality of love.

Love's devotional aspect manifests in every act in which something is given up or in which a living being directs itself to a purpose, activity or person outside of itself. Whether applied to secular or spiritual affairs, this sacrificial element of love constitutes a cosmic law unto itself, the divine law of sacrifice. Herein lies a clue to the power and the mystery of true love.

Possibly the most simple yet complete definition of love is this: the enactment of all of God's divine laws in unison to perfection. This description of love is revealed in Jesus' remark, "If you keep my commandments, you will abide in my love, even as I have kept my Father's commandments and abide in His love." From this viewpoint it is easy to associate the attachment component of love with the divine laws of oneness, integration and attraction. Love's component of affection, whether it leads to impassioned emotion resulting in sexual exchange, or to great works of art, is linked to the divine law of creation.

Strong affection for or attachment or devotion to Spirit, a person or persons, an organization or a cause, or to life in any or all of nature's kingdoms originates in cosmic law as Principle Itself. Each single act of true love embodies elements drawn from all of Spirit's laws: oneness, individuality, polarity, creation, integration, transmutation, sacrifice, equality, give-and-take, free will, noninterference, order, cause and effect, reincarnation, growth and evolution, attraction and repulsion, righteousness, example, balance and harmony, compensation, life, and perfection.

Jesus illuminated the greatest expression of love: "There is no greater love than this, that a man lay down his life for the sake of his friends."

Human history is replete with examples of such love. In the world of nature, ecologists and animal behaviorists question whether they can truly ascertain the motives of animal acts. However, the effects of those actions unquestionably can be known. In this sense, the scientific community has applied Jesus' rule for discernment, "You will know them by their fruits." In place of the word *love,* scientists use the concept of altruism to describe the extensive examples in the animal kingdom of unselfish behavior for the welfare of others.

Sharing food, warning others of danger, adopting orphans, and defending young, territory or colony are altruistic acts performed on a grand scale among animal species. They are fulfilled every day–to the detriment of individual survival–when parents, especially mothers, raise their young. Used to thwart hive-robbers, the barbed hook on the sting of the honeybee can rarely be withdrawn; thus, to a honeybee defense is virtually unsurvivable. The supreme sacrifice of life to defend colonies against larger (and, relatively speaking, gigantic) predators is common to ants, termites, wasps and other social insects.

Charles Darwin, the English natural scientist who first described the theory of evolution, had an explanation for how altruistic parental behavior could survive from generation to generation. In *The Oxford Companion to Animal Behavior,* Richard Dawkins summarizes Darwin's theory:

"Offspring whose lives are saved by parental care tend to inherit the tendency to care for their own young when the time comes. Individuals with a hereditary tendency to starve their offspring would be likely to starve to death before they were old enough to have selfish offspring. Putting the same point in genetic terms, genes for parental care tend to be contained in the bodies of the young saved by the parental care. Genes for parental care therefore tend to increase in frequency relative to genes for selfishness towards offspring."

Scientific discoveries since Darwin's time have shown that this is an oversimplified theory. However, by proposing that selfishness writes itself out of the genetic record by the law of evolution, which we know to be a divine law, Darwin suggests ascent to higher life expression results from behavior in concord with divine law.

Many instances of altruism in nature are actually forms of symbiosis: the living together of organisms of different species for their mutual benefit. This form of love occurs among plants, between plants and animals, and among animals. Furthermore, the relationship can be between individuals, between individuals and societies, and between entire societies. The divine law of give-and-take is in full evidence here, rendering yet another example of the integrated activity of cosmic laws to produce true love.

Through the divine law of love, God created us to be love in action. In a channeled communication on November 5, 1969, Archangel Uriel explained the divine reality of man as love: "My function and purpose are as the guardian of that which is the most precious part of your total being: your spiritual Self. . . . This I Am identity or Self cannot be shed, cannot be transferred, cannot be deadened, as it exists eternally in God or Creative Energy, the principle of life, light, truth. It is the love aspect of God.

"What has been expressed by the light and the truth becomes love. Light is the feminine aspect or the enlightenment of God.

Truth is the principle or the law. Love is the expression of this Energy. So the love of God, which is your I Am consciousness or spiritual Self, is formed eternally from the beginning and never can be dissolved in any way, shape or form. Therefore mankind, which was created equal and whole in the I Am Self, became a physical form and personality in order to experience all three aspects of his Creator: light, truth and love."

Humankind's very essence is love; therefore, one would expect it to be the easiest of Spirit's laws to express. Paradoxically, it is not, as we all know only too well. In a communication on April 16, 1958, Jesus touched on this incongruity:

"It is easy to love when you are loved, but difficult to love when you are hated or misused or ignored. This temptation is the easiest one to which to submit. Those who appear to you in unkindness, inconsideration, boorishness, lack of understanding are your tempters. If you can accept them as God's children and love them in return for their ill will and their hatred, then you can face the world as one of enlightenment. Every step of the disciple's path is fraught with this particular temptation, for you are never universally loved, understood or accepted."

In northern India the Buddha taught virtually the same message: " 'Look how he abused me and beat me, how he threw me down and robbed me.' Live with such thoughts and you live in hate. 'Look how he abused me and beat me, how he threw me down and robbed me.' Abandon such thoughts, and live in love. In this world hate never yet dispelled hate. Only love dispels hate. This is the law, ancient and inexhaustible."

In Palestine Jesus instructed likewise to all those who would listen: "Love your enemies and do good to those who hate you, and bless those who curse you, and pray for those who compel you to carry burdens. And to him who strikes you on the cheek, offer to him the other; and to him who takes away your robe, do not refuse your shirt also. Give to every one who asks you; and from him who takes away what is yours, do not demand it back again. Just as you want men to do to you, do to them likewise.

"For if you love those who love you, what is your blessing? For even sinners love those who love them. And if you do good only to those who do good to you, what is your blessing? For sinners also do the same. And if you lend only to him from whom you expect to be paid back, what is your blessing? For sinners also lend to sinners, to be paid back likewise.

"But love your enemies and do good to them, and lend and do not cut off any man's hope; so your reward will increase and you will become sons of the Highest; for He is gracious to the wicked and the cruel. Be therefore merciful, as your Father also is merciful. Judge not, and you will not be judged; condemn not, and you will not be condemned; forgive, and you will be forgiven."

Even though we were created by Spirit's love for the purpose of loving, humankind has been unable to fulfill that purpose because of selfishness. Man utilizes the divine law of love for self-power and self-gain. The use of spiritual laws for self-centered purposes is man's original sin and the cause of his fall from spiritual grace.

Lord Chamuel, Archangel of the Third Ray of Personal Love and Feeling, explained this in more detail in a communication on October 26, 1971: "When the desire is altruistic there are no problems in your evolutionary pattern and progress. When [your desires] are unselfish or to be returned unto the cosmic pattern of creation, they require little or no supervision, for you are in the divine grace and the grip of your own spirituality and creative seed of knowledge. But when you recognize this power, this knowledge and this activity and erroneously proceed to disassociate it with the divine head or Source, you become misinformed, mismanaged and filled with the mischief of your own creative ideas, purposes and plans. . . .

"For all forces which turn away from the source of light, falling in love with their own powers that are ever with them and never can be withdrawn from them—for they are created of the one Source; and energy cannot be destroyed, it just can be reformulated and remanipulated—the destiny of these sources and forces which are in error is to be recaptured, rehabilitated, resuscitated back into the light and the love of God, which are eternal.

"We ask now how this can be done. It can only be done through the Third Ray aspect, which is love. Love, which is the key to all, is that which shall return the self-love into the selfless love from which it originally was created. Love must conquer in this respect, for it was in the area of love that the fall occurred. Love, then, must be the activity, in its proper and true light, that rehabilitates that which erred in the first place."

In the same communication Archangel Chamuel points to the Golden Rule, which derives from the divine law of equality, as one of the signal keys to living the divine law of love: "You must share, and share alike. You must be responsible for and love all equally to that which you love most dearly in yourself. What is it that man, or any life form, loves most dearly within himself, but the Life Source Itself? Living, thinking, feeling: this is life and energy, or God within you, expressing outwardly, that you love, that you cherish, and that you must love and cherish in all other things as much as you do in yourself. When you can share this equally and care about it equally for all other forms of life as you care about it for yourself, you will rehabilitate all other forms of life."

One of the most beautifully instructive accounts of love in religious literature was written to the Christian community in Corinth by the apostle Paul. It was inspired by love as exemplified and taught by Jesus: "Though I speak with the tongues of men and of angels, and have not love in my heart, I am become as sounding brass or a tinkling cymbal. And though I have the gift of prophecy, and understand all mysteries and all knowledge; and though I have all faith, so that I could remove mountains, and have not love in my heart, I am nothing. And though I bestow all my goods to feed the poor, and though I give my body to be burned, and have not love in my heart, I gain nothing.

"Love is long-suffering and kind; love does not envy; love does not make a vain display of itself, and does not boast, does not behave itself unseemly, seeks not its own, is not easily provoked, thinks no evil; rejoices not over iniquity, but rejoices in the truth; bears all things, believes all things, hopes all things, endures all things. Love never fails. . . . And now abide faith, hope, love, these three; but the greatest of these is love."

The divine law of love is the key to comprehending our purpose, our very existence, wherever we live throughout the universe. Truly, by upholding this law we unlock the doorway to a new level of existence and a new way of life on Earth. As Sananda-Jesus, Prince of Earth, revealed in a communication on October 20, 1969, love is the key to the Second Coming: "Be that love force and use that love force in every conceivable situation. You have this power and will in you at all times. It is a matter of using it at will.

"If you will, use love as divinely guided and directed in whatever measure you deem appropriate; but use it. If you cannot love a person or situation as it is, love that person and situation as it is meant to be or as you desire it to become. All is in a state of becoming. Therefore, what is the highest and greatest or most desirable activity, but love? So, become love in action. That is your scheme and your activity of future projects.

"I ask and seek this in my name. For as I return unto the force field of Earth over a period of short years, I can only return through love and by the love power invoked for me and my mission concerning Earth. Those who cannot love me by name must transmute these feelings of negativity, and love me for the works or desires of upliftment for the race which are done in my name. This is an example of the right use of the power of love. For to love and to bring love energy into any human situation is to equalize it with the Father-Mother Creative Principle. The equalizing both balances negativity into positive response and causes a new form to become manifested in and through the person or conditions experiencing this particular vibration. . . .

"You are not to be concerned with doing this, as you do not do anything. The law or Lord God does all things. You are the focal points of energy and creation through which He works. Therefore, make yourselves agreeable and available for Him to do this work. You do this by becoming love in action. By bringing love into focus and demonstration throughout the Earth and in all parts of Earth form (and this is the secret, the key, the need), the time comes for this energy pattern to materialize on Earth. For as you create this formula for me and my works and my mission, you create a new heaven on a new Earth, and all will be made new."

CREATION

God said, "Let there be light." And there is light, in every mind, in every heart and in every soul on Earth. As a cocreator with Spirit, man creates without ceasing because creation is a constantly active spiritual principle. Humankind's highest expression of this cosmic law is to create in the same way that the Creator does.

Creation is a sacred act, for at the heart of all creative activity are divine laws. We normally associate creation with physical laws governing biology, physics and other sciences; also, with inspired thoughts and feelings that give rise to the creative arts and music. But they are merely outward, tangible manifestations of inner, spiritual principles.

Without God as divine laws, there would be no creativity. There would be no creation. We would not exist. Therefore, creative acts become holy (that is, wholesome) only when spiritual principles are adopted. Once the sacredness of the creative act is established, procreation of life assumes the holiness that Spirit originally intended. This is true in every endeavor where creativity is employed.

Good. Order. Divine. Put the first letters of these words together and what do we have? *GOD.* In some translations of the Torah, the first words in Genesis are "When God began to create . . ." rather than "In the beginning God created . . ." Hasidic teachers preferred the phrase "When God began to create" because to them it indicated that God created in a particular order. Is there an ordered set of principles that comprise the divine law of creation?

Archangel Jophiel of this solar system's government confirms that there is. In a communication on October 24, 1971, describing the activity of the Seven Rays of Life, he explained the divine procedure of creation: "We will teach you about the creation of form out of matter. . . . God is all that is, and in Him or It, which is Creative Substance, come all the aspects, the elements and the activities which are divine, unchangeable and spiritual law. It is based on mathematical precision, as you would think in terms of scientific exactness. . . .

"As we speak we precipitate these laws into action; and hope and trust, and protect you, that you will use this spiritual, scientific formula to bring about that desired result in your own lives for the good of all that comes under your influence. . . .

"The first law or light of God is energy. . . . It is the idea to create, to be. . . . From the second aspect comes . . . thought or mind in motion, creating and bringing forth the third, which is love, the love of God. . . . This triune action had manifested, had crystallized and had equaled the fourth. For the two primary aspects, which are Father-Mother God, masculine-feminine polarities, creating love, developed a fourth true and sound form in matter. . . .

"This foundation or these four corners create or sustain all life form throughout all universes. But standing upon this foursquare, we put the unity of purpose and the integrating of all these principles under the Fifth Ray or aspect; . . . under the elohim of integrating substance and thought, activity and love. Building upon this, we then transmute, refine and purify all that has been gained and has been gathered by this activity, this thought. The sixth aspect of God in action is the transmuting flame. . . . We come to the seventh [the resting or peace aspect, the love of Spirit Itself and the love of doing Spirit's work], . . . which completes all that has gone before it. . . . Nothing else is needed.

"If you can understand all of these principles involved, the aspects of God in and through all creation—divine law, and love and light combined upon a solid foundation of the first four activities— you yourselves can create any idea, any principle, any love and bring it into full manifestation and spiritualized creativity. Let this ever be your law in practice. Let this ever be your procedure."

The first step of creation is the idea to create, to be. This includes both the pure, raw, creative substance of God and the laws that govern it. Divine energy and divine laws produce life and the will to create new life.

Shakespeare's Hamlet said, "To be, or not to be: that is the question." That will always be humankind's question. Will we choose life and choose to continue with our lives, come what may? Will we choose to live according to spiritual principles? Will we acknowledge that God is the source of all the energy we use? Spirit gives us the freedom of will to resolve these questions however we want. But whatever we decide, there will be either favorable or unfavorable consequences. For creation, like free will and cause and effect, is an ever-active cosmic law. With unparalleled historical unanimity, the truly great spiritual teachers of this world have taught: Choose life. Choose righteousness. Choose love.

The second step is mind or intelligence, the thoughts of God. In the biblical creation story God said, "Let there be light"; and there was light. Dr. George M. Lamsa, an authority on ancient Eastern manuscripts and founder of the Aramaic Bible Society, explains the term *light* in his book *Old Testament Light*: "*Bahra*, 'shining,' light in this instance, means enlightenment. That is, the light and the knowledge of God and moral law. Darkness in Aramaic is symbolical of ignorance, superstition, and evil."

Comprehension of cosmic principles engenders wisdom. Aristotle closed his first chapter of *Metaphysics* by writing, "Clearly then wisdom is knowledge about certain causes and principles." Thought brings spiritual laws and energies of Divine Mind into life. Gautama Buddha said, "Our life is shaped by our mind; we become what we think."

The third step of creation is feeling the love of God. Spirit's energy and laws wedded to wisdom and understanding create the highest desire in creation: love. Divine love is inherent within every child of God. For us to become unemotional, devoid of desires or detached from life, as certain philosophies teach, goes against our divine nature. We need only eliminate all motivating desires that are less than love.

As it is written in the *Brihadaranyaka* Upanishad, "When all the knots that strangle the heart are loosened, the mortal becomes immortal, here in this very life. As the skin of a snake is sloughed onto an anthill, so does the mortal body fall; but the Self, freed from the body, merges in Brahman, infinite life, eternal light."

Life, light and love: the first three steps of creation are the holy trinity. After these three activities physical form appears. In the primary scripture of Taoism, the *Tao te ching,* which means "the way of virtue," creation is described this way: "The Tao begot one. One begot two. Two begot three. And three begot the ten thousand things."

The fourth step is manifestation, myriads of manifestations! This step requires using elements of the first three steps equally in every conception. Equal proportions of energy and law, enlightened thoughts and wisdom, with love as the prime motivating desire, will produce true and sound products every time.

The fifth creative step incorporates each new creation with the rest of the cosmos. Spirit is always at one with Its creation, and this oneness is maintained by the divine law of integration. Whenever new life forms, knowledge or beneficial productions of any kind are conceived, the law of integration synthesizes each with all/All.

The sixth step is change; specifically, change that refines, purifies and transmutes whatever is created. God's original creation was not only good, it was perfect. Yet, all the diversity of life that God produced did not remain in a condition of static perfection, because the sixth creative act is the divine law of transmutation.

Change is everlasting. It is divinely ordained. It is the cause of the divine dissatisfaction within us that compels us to improve ourselves and all we create.

The seventh step of creation is divine love, rest and peace. God "rested on the seventh day." Adhering to the six previous steps creates love for God and for the magnificent way in which God's principles and energies work together. Rest is possible in the seventh step through the knowledge that life is being lived righteously. This knowledge imparts peace that can only be described as divine.

These are the seven steps or laws of creation. Obviously, without God we can do nothing. Confucius, who without exaggeration can be said to have molded over two thousand years of Chinese civilization, stated: "I transmit but do not create." Christ Jesus, whose impact on the world the past two thousand years is impossible to measure, said: "The words that I speak, I do not speak of myself; but my Father who abides with me does these works."

Both knew that a true understanding of the relationship between God and a servant of God is fundamental to the proper expression of the divine law of creation. We are cocreators with Spirit and the sole creator of nothing.

The following is a list of the seven steps of creation, each followed by an affirmation:

1. I *will.* I will to do God's will.
2. I *know.* I will know the laws of God and use them wisely.
3. I *desire.* I will desire to love only as God loves.
4. I *create.* I will create only as my I Am Self directs; with equal amounts of life, light and love.
5. I *unite.* I will unite all the good that I create with the rest of creation.
6. I *change.* I will change, refine and purify all that I produce.
7. I *rest.* I will rest by working in the peace of divine love.

All of God's creations are immaculately conceived. The entire race of man is an immaculate conception of Spirit. We each have the power to conceive immaculately, for God's life, light, love and law are within us. So, let us cocreate with God on Earth even as we do in heaven. By so doing, the re-formation of Earth will be conceived and brought forth in purity and love.

INTEGRATION

In the Bible, the prophet Isaiah proclaimed, "The whole earth is full of His glory." In the Koran, Muhammad wrote, "Wherever you turn, there is God's face." In the Hindu scripture, the *Bhagavad Gita,* it is written, "You are behind me and in front of me; I bow to You on every side. Your power is immeasurable. You pervade everything; You are everything."

Aren't the words from these three scriptures beautiful? Wouldn't it be wonderful to wake up every morning and live in such oneness with God and all life that we could see God's magnificence in everything? Wouldn't it be marvelous to be able to realize so acutely the influence of divine laws in the actions of mankind on this planet that we could say, "Everywhere I look, I see God's face"?

What these scriptures describe is not fantasy, but a cosmic viewpoint of reality and of our future. Such a view of life becomes possible when we more fully understand and use the great and all-encompassing divine law of integration. Countless people throughout history have recorded similar experiences and perceptions of God's presence in every atom of creation. Many of us who are in spiritual work also on occasion have felt this sublime oneness with our Creator and creation.

Although such experiences may seem to be impermanent, it is not Spirit's union with us that comes and goes. It is our conscious awareness of Spirit's unity that fluctuates. The solution to this problem of separation is in grasping the law of integration and never letting go. Never letting go of this fundamental truth, no matter what happens to us in life and no matter what divisiveness and disintegration we see in the world around us.

On May 13, 1964, Hilarion, Chohan of the Fifth Ray of Integration and Unity, communicated the spiritual meaning of integration:

"Integration . . . refers absolutely to our sense of unity and oneness with all life. . . . Integration is that sphere of activity within the whole that allows it to continue in one body and denies or offsets the tremendous sweep of separation during the era of marks and the signs that call for elimination of error and defining of truth."

So, integration and unity, though they are similar in meaning, are not synonymous. In terms of cosmic principles, unity is another name for the law of oneness. Oneness is a fundamental law that describes reality, what permanently exists. Oneness does not change. God, the Creator of all that is and who is in all things, is forever in a state of perfect union. In reality, no person or thing can completely separate itself from God. Nor is there anything that has a separate existence from God.

Integration, on the other hand, is the activity or the process that unites, incorporates or reformulates things into a whole. Just because the oneness of God does not change does not mean that change is not going on within Divine Unity. On the contrary, there are vast and continual changes instigated and justified by other divine laws, such as transmutation, and growth and evolution. Integration, as Hilarion said, is the activity within the whole that allows oneness to continue.

Integration is like a powerful cosmic glue that permits change and, yet, at the same time does not disturb cohesion. From a mortal perspective, it may seem that the world and maybe even our lives are falling apart; that the glue is somehow coming unstuck. But from a cosmic perspective founded on spiritual principles, just the opposite is true.

God's face, in this instance meaning God's laws being used by humankind, can be seen in the great advances in global telecommunications, networking, worldwide economic interdependence, interdisciplinary scientific commissions, environmental conferences, ecumenical religious organizations and conferences, advances in the holistic approach to medicine, and international responses to segregated societies and human rights infractions. The world is not coming apart. The world is coming together.

In these end days before the Second Coming, our challenge and our opportunity are to bring to bear every spiritual power and soul talent with which we are blessed in order to radiate out the energy of integration to humanity. According to God's will, we invoke integration, so that the changes which must occur within man's consciousness be done with the least amount of disharmony and imbalance.

On February 6, 1963, Hilarion relayed this insight on how to establish a force field of integration for this planet: "I wish you would meditate and think upon the growth of your own history and see that it has been a struggle toward unification, a struggle toward integration. I wish you would realize that everything having to do with the sciences and the arts has been toward this struggle, toward this goal, of integrating the whole man. All of your philosophy, all of your psychology that have been brought forth since the beginning have been in the process of integrating this principle. It is a unifying idea: bring about unity, bring about oneness, prove our interdependence, and practice it in one form or another."

The activity of integration in the religious history of mankind is nothing short of phenomenal. What proof is there? Judaism, Christianity and Islam, the three religions that most fully embrace monotheism, the belief in one God, originated in cultures whose people believed and worshipped many gods at the same time. These religions were conceived in response to polytheism.

Between 1700 and 1500 B.C., the same process occurred when Zarathustra integrated all of the Indo-Iranian deities into one supreme God, Ahura Mazda. Again, integration manifested in Egypt when Pharaoh Amunhotep IV, around 1375 B.C., rescinded the authority of all the old Egyptian gods and instead raised up the one God, Aton.

In the history of Sufism, the mystical branch of Islam, one individual towers above all the rest: Ibn 'Arabi (1165–1240). His genius lay in his ability to synthesize into a comprehensible whole all of the mystical teachings of Sufism. His central concept was called *wahdat al-wujud,* which means "unity of being."

One final example: amid the religious upheaval in India in the late 1400s and early 1500s the great Guru Nanak integrated the Hindu form of monotheism with the monotheism of Islam, creating a new monotheistic form: Sikhism.

The history of Eastern and Western philosophy also is full of examples of integration. In the fourth century B.C., Plato advanced the unity of the Good, and linked the Good with God. Aristotle's First Mover or First Cause is the eternal, one, changeless God, who also is good and is united with the physical world.

Plotinus, the founder of Neoplatonism in the third century A.D., integrated the wisdom of Plato and Aristotle and combined it with his own mystical experiences of oneness. His works and those of Plato had a profound influence on the medieval Islamic, Judaic and Christian thinkers for centuries. No small wonder, as one can see in this extract from his *Enneads,* an exhortation to integrate with Spirit, Principle Itself:

"We are in search of unity; we are to come to know the principle of all, the Good and First; therefore we may not stand away from the realm of Firsts and lie prostrate among the lasts: we must strike for those Firsts, rising from things of sense which are the lasts. Cleared of all evil in our intention towards The Good, we must ascend to the Principle within ourselves; from many, we must become one; only so do we attain to knowledge of that which is Principle and Unity."

The foremost Hindu philosopher was the ninth-century mystic Shankara. He consolidated the greatest writings of the ancient Indian sages and proposed an original philosophy of the Absolute so powerful that today it stands as a model of monistic thinking; that is, a philosophical system that emphasizes the oneness of reality.

Finally, there is the greatest synthesizer in the history of Chinese philosophy, Chu Hsi. He lived in the twelfth century A.D. and integrated the works of earlier giants Confucius and Mencius with his own magnificent thoughts. The resulting *Four Books,* a compendium of ethical and moral teachings, became the basis of civil service examinations in China for almost six hundred years, from 1313 to 1905. One of his major concepts was that the Great Ultimate, or God, in the universe and in each individual thing, is never different and never separate. For centuries, Chu Hsi's philosophical works dominated Chinese, Korean and Japanese thought.

These are only a few of the countless examples of integration in religion and philosophy. The same extensive expression of the law of integration can be found throughout the history of science, the arts, medicine and all of the other fields of human endeavor. The basic effect this divine principle has on our lives is that it unifies us with God, with our own I Am Self, and with all Spirit's children, both human and of nature. Integration enables us to perceive God's laws, life, enlightenment and love in the world and universe around us.

God's law of integration disallows eternal separation or damnation. There never has been an instant in our eternal lives wherein God has forsaken any one of us. Let us obliterate this false belief forever from the race consciousness of mankind.

For anyone who wants to integrate or reintegrate with God, Christ Jesus says that we first need simply to "ask, and it shall be given to you; seek, and you shall find; knock, and it shall be opened to you. For whoever asks, receives; and he who seeks, finds; and to him who knocks, the door is opened."

TRANSMUTATION

Transmutation is one of the most important aspects of all activity, since the manifestations of Creative Life Force can never remain stationary or stagnant. Divine Mind keeps Its creations gradually evolving and dissolving and remanifesting into greater spiritual expression, for this is the nature of Divine Energy and the purpose of divine love.

Transmutation is not a commonly used word. In science or alchemy it usually refers to chemical transmutation. But, as exemplified in channelings through me, masters on the highest spiritual planes select the word *transmutation* in favor of its synonyms, *transformation* and *change*. This is particularly true when they speak in terms of divine law and divine attributes of life, the Seven Rays of Life.

The reason for this is that the word *transmute* comes from Latin words meaning "to change across." Transmutation denotes change from one nature, form, species, condition or substance into another. It is more than just changing the outward appearance of something, which is usually spoken of as a transformation. Transmutation means that there is an inward change as well.

Because the word *change* has so many meanings, it would be difficult to know exactly what a spiritual master would mean if he were to refer only to the law of change. Divine transmutation is pure change, change that makes pure. It is change so complete that an existing condition will "cross over" and become a completely new one. Old forms and substances actually "pass over" and become new form and substance.

Just as each individual's free will is made possible by God's divine will, and our personal love expression is just a part of the total love of Spirit, all change is made possible by the law of transmutation. As stated above, Spirit can never remain stationary or still. Therefore, whether it be a change from a mortal consciousness and flesh body into Christ consciousness and the light body, or a change of position in time and space, such as driving across town in a car, the transmutation principle is involved.

Personal examples of transmutation can easily be found in our diaries and photo albums. But to drive home the importance of this law, we would need to do what even God is incapable of doing: switch off the law as if we would switch off a light bulb.

What would happen if we could? What would happen if all change, all transmutation were to cease? The answer is that nothing would happen. Nothing would ever happen again. There would be universal suspended animation. Imagine all physical motion stopping forever. All vibrations and frequencies, sound waves, light radiation and electrical impulses would freeze. The only sounds and sights that we would hear and see would be those that remained with us at the moment transmutation ceased.

Time would stop. Physical, mental and emotional development would stop. All changes of mind and heart would stop. If we were hating something or someone when transmutation ended, we would remain in a perpetual state of hate. That would be awful. Change is good.

This is a real-life example of Spirit's omnipresence and omnipotence throughout Its creation, in terms of this one cosmic law. It is not a fantasy, parable or allegory.

Just as profound is this information dictated by me in the consciousness of my high Self, Nada, on June 26, 1966: "Life principle operates both negatively and positively. We have what we call life and death. We have what we call growth and destruction. We have transmutation, and that is the proper word for death and destruction. For life must transmute all forms of its creation; otherwise, you would have creation upon creation and confusion and chaos. Whereas if you have life that transmutes and grows, you have everlasting, eternal immortality of energy. This is truth and cannot be looked upon in any other manner but in this way. Nothing else is acceptable, nothing else is real, nothing else lives."

Without transmutation nothing lives. Without transitions in life, eternal life is impossible. These concepts are of tremendous importance in our attitude toward changing ourselves and humanity. Transmutation is necessary for our daily life. It gives us the ability to change from mortal consciousness and physical existence to spiritual consciousness and light-body form. This law is indispensable for our personal second coming of I Am Self beingness and for the Second Coming of Sananda-Jesus, Prince and planetary ruler of Earth. We should love it.

And yet, individually and as a race, we often avoid or oppose positive change. We fear death. We resist the law of transmutation. In spite of our rational intentions, we resist and fear God in us and His will for us–the very same One who gives us life.

During the Exodus from Egypt, the children of Israel constantly

45

complained to Moses and Aaron about their change of life, even though God sustained them with miracle after miracle. Once, as they were blaming the two patriarchs yet again, Moses revealed to them the underlying truth of their dissent, saying, "As for us [Moses and Aaron], what are we? Your murmurings are not against us but against the Lord."

The struggle with the laws of God did not end with Moses and the Israelites. Blaming God and resisting and fearing the Lord, the laws of Spirit, continue today. What are we to do? The answer is to embrace wholeheartedly this divine law and transmute ourselves. We begin with ourselves because we truly cannot change anyone else. We can influence others by what we think, say and do, and thereby give them an example to follow. But we can secure only our own transmutation.

This is what the Israelites did before the Exodus. Some Jewish teachers claim that of all the miracles performed in ancient Egypt and the wilderness–the plagues, the parting of the Red Sea, the manna from heaven, and all the other great changes of nature–the greatest miracle was each Israelite's change of heart and mind that was a part of the first Passover. It was a change so powerful and so great that in the face of utter annihilation by the Egyptians a whole people fearlessly worshipped the One God and left for a new life.

What they had and what we all need now in our own changes and transmutations is faith in God, faith in the laws of God that can never do us harm if we will but embrace them, understand them and use them.

On October 21, 1971, Lord Zadkiel, Archangel of the Sixth Ray of Transmutation, channeled the attitude we should cultivate about transmutation:

"Many choices will be given in these end days and during this purification time. It should not be looked upon as an unpleasant task and a difficult one. It really should be looked upon with great pleasure. You should strive within to make it one of the most enjoyable and exciting moments of your entire spiritual experience, . . . because it is that moment when you utilize every power, every intui-

46

tion, every intellectual, knowledgeable point and say: this will serve me in my ongoing stages and can be productive for the good of man and for my own spiritual mission and role upon the Earth and in the times to come after this mission and this life experience; or, it will not serve. If it will not serve, then it should be without difficulty, and it should be expedient, to eliminate it."

Although there are pain and suffering associated with cruci-fixions, purification and refinement, the fruits of transmutation are necessary for resurrections to occur. Although during times of for-giveness and repentance there are mourning and sorrow, these are lawful activities of transmutation that are necessary to bring about a true Day of Atonement, at-onement with God.

When the Israelites finished building the second Temple in Jerusalem after their exile in Babylon, they renewed their covenant with God by reading the laws of God. They were, as mankind today is or will be, distressed at hearing the demands of the laws and regretted all of their shortcomings. They mourned and wept bitterly.

Upon witnessing the people mourn, Nehemiah, the high priest, gave them a pleasant message, just as Lord Zadkiel emphasized joy over sorrow. Nehemiah said, "Go your way, eat and drink and send portions to them for whom nothing is prepared; for this day is holy to the Lord; and do not be sad, for this is a day of joy of the Lord, and He will be your strength."

The message is clear. When we uphold the Lord, the laws of God, in our temple—that is, in our hearts, minds, bodies and souls—it is a holy time and we should be filled with joy. Because we willingly have eliminated our fear and resistance, the Lord, the cosmic laws, will be our strength.

SACRIFICE

Somewhere on this planet right now someone is making a sacrifice for another or is performing a ritual of sacrifice to a supernatural being. In fact, since the Stone Age the race of man uninterruptedly has enacted this divine law. Sacrifice is known to have been performed by man well before the earliest known written documents, of Sumerian origin, recorded some five thousand years ago.

Anthropologists and religious scholars have been able to deduce by the placement of bones, stones and other artifacts that primitive, Upper Paleolithic, Cro-Magnon man participated in acts of sacrifice ten to twelve thousand years ago. Some experts argue for, and others against, the "religious character" of Middle Paleolithic evidence left by Neanderthal man thirty-five to seventy-five thousand years ago.

The word *sacrifice* comes from two Latin words, *sacer*, "sacred," and *facere*, "to make"; hence, to make sacred. Sacrifice means to offer anything to a deity out of respect or for goodwill to continue. It also means to give up, destroy or forgo something of value for the sake of something that has greater value or that has a more pressing claim.

On October 28, 1971, Archangel Uriel, of the solar system government, gave the full spiritual definition of sacrifice: "Not many are able to put themselves in the position where they devote and donate every ounce of their spiritual affairs to a single individual or purpose which is not of their own evolvement and development. Only when self-sacrifice is entered into the picture of spiritually unfolded consciousnesses can we see the full magnificence and the full manifestation of the Christ Son in action."

Addressing all souls of the race of man, she states further: "They cannot fulfill their own functions and exercise their own highest aspects unless they learn to use the sacrificial element within themselves for the good of one outside of themselves. This is truth. This is how truth is served. This is the law and the manifestation of that law in any plane of spiritual action."

Mircea Eliade, one of the world's finest religious historians, speaks of the same conception of sacrifice and describes it in reference to Stone Age people in the first volume of his work *A History of Religious Ideas:* "In short, the 'sacred' is an element in the structure of consciousness and not a stage in the history of consciousness. On the most archaic levels of culture, *living, considered as being human,* is in itself a *religious act,* for food-getting, sexual life, and work have a sacramental value. . . .

"For some two million years, the Paleanthropians lived by hunting; fruits, roots, mollusks, and so on, gathered by the women and children, did not suffice to insure the survival of the species. . . . But the ceaseless pursuit and killing of game ended by creating a unique system of relationships between the hunter and the slain animals. . . .

"In the last analysis, this 'mystical solidarity' with the game reveals the kinship between human societies and the animal world. To kill the hunted beast or, later, the domestic animal is equivalent to a 'sacrifice' in which the victims are interchangeable. We must add that all these concepts came into existence during the last phases of the process of hominization. They are still active—altered, revalorized, camouflaged—millennia after the disappearance of the Paleolithic civilizations."

Compared to modern-day man, early primitive man was obviously of more limited awareness and intelligence. So, what is the significance of the fact that he was enacting this cosmic law, and who knows, maybe doing so more consciously than many people today? It means that no matter who we are, no matter how much we know or do not know, as children of God we have our Creator's divine spark within us, which consists of Spirit as divine principles and energies. Cosmic laws are the sacred, spiritual elements that give us life and the capacity to express life divinely.

Indeed, what is most primal in man but the image and energy of Spirit within him? Man's original instincts, his most powerful primal urges, are of Spirit as divine elements within him. To sacrifice, then, to offer or give up some valued thing to God or to others with a more pressing claim, is a primal urge within us that cannot, in the end, be denied. Just witness parents–human or animal–protecting their offspring: when danger strikes suddenly, blindingly quick reflexes act to save the young ones. In such instances, the law of sacrifice is clearly demonstrated.

The Hindu *Chandogya* Upanishad states simply, "Man is sacrifice." If the law of sacrifice is so embodied in us, let us get a clear picture of what to sacrifice and how to sacrifice. Since God created all things perfect and, therefore, holy, we cannot make a tree or a mountain or ourselves more sacred than they or we originally and innately are. Man cannot make God holier than God already is, although God knows we have tried. However, we can correct erroneous thoughts, desires and actions that have caused all of the desecration in the natural world and in mankind.

Often we shy away from acts of sacrifice because we know we are going to suffer some negative consequence. True, we usually do suffer when we sacrifice. But suffering is connected with the error we are trying to remove and not with the principle of sacrifice. There is no intrinsic relationship between suffering and sacrifice. Sacrifice is a divine law of God. God is good and holy and just.

So, it is an error to think that acts of sacrifice cause our suffering. This would be to blame God for our suffering. This is never the case. God is not evil. In truth, we suffer because we do *not* sacrifice; that is to say, we fail to live this divine law by not making all of our thoughts, feelings and actions sacred.

Always we must separate cosmic principles from the evil or the errors that we ourselves commit. What suffering can there be in sacrificing those things in mind, body and soul that prevent us from expressing our Christ nature? What deprivation can there be in following God's will? True suffering and lasting deprivation are produced by continued resistance to cosmic law.

On April 11, 1958, the apostle John channeled sage advice concerning one of the most important aspects of sacrifice: "Not one of us is better or higher than the next, whether he or she is a leader or one being led. For in each is the potential for God realization. We each have the obligation to become Godlike. We each have the obligation, in our preparation and leadership, to bring those behind us up to our level of understanding. So it is with you, so it is with us, so it is with those ahead of us. God is the goal all are trying to reach."

Helping those who have a more pressing claim than we because they are less evolved, willful or bogged down in false beliefs is our spiritual obligation under the law of sacrifice. This law explicitly confirms selflessness. Thus, it directly heals selfishness.

A beautifully poetic description of sacrifice is found in Taoist scripture. Here are two translations of the same verse: "Turning back is how the way moves." "Returning is the motion of the Tao." Turning back–returning to the less advanced and less fortunate–not only is a duty here on Earth but also is the way of the universe.

For those who know this, turning back is not a self-centered act. We return not because we know that humankind can only evolve together as a race, though this is true. We turn back not because we know we will incur good karma by doing so, though this also is true. We sacrifice our energy and incarnation not because we know we will receive more from Spirit than we will ever give, though this, too, is true. We share our lives because we see the needs of others and respond without a thought for ourselves. We sacrifice because it is an integral, inseparable part of our divine nature.

One of the earliest examples of human interaction in the Bible is the allegory of Cain and Abel. Their first acts to God were to sacrifice the fruits of their labor. God was pleased with Abel's sacrifice but found Cain's sacrifice unacceptable. Cain was so upset that he killed Abel, who was his brother.

What was missing in Cain's attempt to make sacred, that is, to sacrifice? Selflessness.

In his subsequent conversation with God, Cain asked, "Am I my brother's keeper?" In other words, "Am I responsible for others?" Cain's beliefs and actions, including his sacrifice, were fundamentally self-centered; in a word, selfish. God therefore was not pleased. Cain's sacrifice would only have been acceptable, had the motive been selfless. This standard holds true for our sacrifices today.

As an exercise in true sacrifice, take one bad habit and sacrifice it; put an end to it. This kind of sacrifice is infinitely more powerful than performing rites involving the killing of other life forms. Let life be sacrosanct. Rather than end an incarnation, be it human, plant or animal, sacrifice *the error within yourself.*

May all people on Earth follow our example. May all children of God sanction only the proper expression of this law. May our lives be a sacrament to God. May our hearts be sacred, our souls be sanctified, and this Earth be a sanctuary of love, peace and brotherhood. The beauty of our sacrificial acts is that we do them not for ourselves only. We do them for all life throughout the cosmos.

EQUALITY

"We hold these truths to be self-evident, that all men are created equal. . . ." Many people around the world are familiar with these words of the Declaration of Independence of the United States of America.

Almost all of us are attracted to the idea of equality. This is because equality is more than just a political idea thought up by moral men and women, or an idea merely related to race, commerce or gender. Equality is a cosmic law, a principle of life of the highest order, which originates in God, not man.

All men are created equal. It is equally true, according to the divine law of equality, that all life forms created by God are equal. This includes angels, devas, animals, plants, minerals and elements. We all are equal in this respect: each living being is created and sustained by the same divine, indwelling positive-negative creative life force of our Father-Mother God.

We also are equal in that each of us has a divinely mandated triune purpose that compels us to live, to think, to feel and to evolve towards ever-greater expressions of love. This is the divine trinity of being, knowing and acting; or in other words, life, light and love. Beyond these, there are real and imagined inequalities. But neither man nor beast, neither death nor destruction of any kind can destroy the divine energy and divine trinity which God has established in each of us, His-Her children.

Before we discuss the inequalities within the race of man, let's look at the relationship between man and nature. The misconception that man is in all ways superior to the other life forms on Earth has contributed heavily to the current desecration of the planet that scientists around the world have revealed and that we cope with daily.

God did create man with greater spiritual consciousness and powers by which to govern or have dominion over the lower kingdoms. But lower does not mean inferior in the sense of being less important or having less value, merit or quality. Mankind must not be less respectful and less appreciative of the life, the enlightenment and the love of any life form. Life, light and love are the inalienable rights endowed by the Creator to each and every being in the universe.

What, then, is the proper way of thinking about our differences with and relationship to the nature kingdoms? Here are two sets of similar ideas from remarkably different sources. The first set is from Archangel Uriel, as channeled by me and published in our texts *Evolution of Man* and *Angels and Man* in 1971 and 1974, respectively. The second set is from a little-known Russian Jew, Rabbi Schneur Zalman, published in his book, *An Anthology of Sayings,* in 1796.

First, Lord Uriel: "All source is one and all energy force is the same. However, the degree by which that energy force is utilized makes for the difference in levels of consciousness, functions, services and responsibilities." She states further: "So, never look down upon any other species, no matter how confined it may be in its expression of now, and see it not in this same energy or expanding-out consciousness, for it is so. Some take longer and have less intelligence and force and energy to drive it forth."

Now in Rabbi Zalman's words: "The Infinite Being fills all worlds and provides the Life Force for them all. . . . The essence of the Infinite Being is exactly the same in the lowest worlds as it is in the highest. . . . The only difference between the highest spiritual worlds and the lowest ones involves the transmission of the Life Force. . . .

"The higher worlds receive this in a somewhat more revealed manner than the lower ones. The entities that exist in each world then receive it, each one according to its own particular nature and strength. In each case, this depends on the particular mode through which the Infinite Being transmits Life Force to each one and illuminates it."

This is an excellent example of how truth, though it be revealed and stated differently, remains the same through time and place.

Finally, let's turn our attention back to an archangel, Lord Chamuel, who, on October 26, 1971, communicated the solution to man's failure to apply the law of equality in his relationship with all kingdoms of life: "The higher Self, the spiritual goals and missions of any force are those that speak of equal sharing, equal opportunities, equitable arrangements of all that exists for the good of all who are expressing in the same area of development. In the broadest sense this does include every life form and every element.

"But when one superimposes over another or shares only an insignificant amount of his bounty with another, you have much imbalance in the area of expression, mentally, emotionally and spiritually speaking. These imbalances then create other imbalances. Until you bring about a balance on Earth in these things, you never can create a truly spiritualized energy comparison and bring the entire species of man, with his brethren of the other dimensions and the other kingdoms elsewhere, into a profitable and sharing arrangement which will enhance all equally and will develop all simultaneously. That must be the purpose of any dimension of activity. It must be the purpose of any planet that is expressing anywhere."

Throughout our history, to our credit, we have been concerned with the law of equality, though we may have called it by another name. One such name is the Golden Rule and it has been expressed in many different ways: Do unto others as you would have others do unto you. Or as K'ung Fu-tzu, Confucius, taught, "A man of humanity, wishing to establish his own character, also establishes the character of others, and wishing to be prominent himself, also helps others to be prominent."

But even though we may know the Golden Rule, let's not fool ourselves by thinking it is easy to live that way. In a channeling on April 16, 1958, reviewing the three major temptations that all of us face, Jesus had the law of equality first on the list: "One of the temptations is spiritual pride. To think or to feel one is elevated above one's brother or sister in spiritual knowledge or favor is against the divine law of equality. All men are created equal. What you have gained your sisters and brothers are capable of gaining, and shall gain, in their turn. Therefore, it is erroneous to put one's self above the crowd as having achieved something the others have not achieved. For time is the only factor between you and them."

In the same way that our level of being is more expansive than that of the nature kingdoms, there are also gradations in evolvement within the race of man. All of us are not equal in spiritual achievement. Decision by decision, action by action, throughout our present life and in all our former lifetimes, either we have utilized spiritual energies and opportunities for growth properly or we have frittered them away. Over time it all adds up. This is the truth behind Confucius' statement, "By nature men are alike. Through practice they have become far apart."

One of the main lessons of Jesus' parable of the prodigal son is to love people equally, regardless of what they do. In that parable, even though one son left his father's house and squandered all the inheritance money given to him, the father still loved that son as much as the other son who never left. We can liken this to those who would follow their own self-will, even when it conflicts with spiritual principles. They fritter away Spirit's energy and delay the inheritance of their Christ consciousness and powers. Does Spirit love those people any less? No. So we must love those who are in error as much as those who continue to try their best to do God's will.

Time and again throughout history, people have restated the interconnection between the law of equality and the law of love. For example, in ancient China there was a period known as the Warring States, which began in 480 B.C. Much like a microcosm of today's global condition, states were fighting each other because rulers were trying to dominate one another and become even more powerful. This resulted in social chaos and widespread poverty and hunger among the people.

Out of this hostile environment came a military leader and philosopher, Mo Tzu, with a solution: universal love. Explaining his conception of "all-embracing" love, Mo Tzu said: "It is to regard other people's countries as one's own. Regard other people's families as one's own. Regard other people's person as one's own.

"Consequently, when feudal lords love one another, they will not fight in the fields. When heads of families love one another, they will not usurp one another. When individuals love one another, they will not injure one another. When ruler and minister love each other, they will be kind and loyal. When father and son love each other, they will be affectionate and filial. When brothers love each other, they will be peaceful and harmonious.

"When all the people in the world love one another, the strong will not overcome the weak, the many will not oppress the few, the rich will not insult the poor, the honored will not despise the humble, and the cunning will not deceive the ignorant."

Over four hundred years after Mo Tzu, in the Middle East, at a dark and tragic hour in Jesus' life, he told his few disciples: "Just as my Father has loved me, I also have loved you; abide in my love. If you keep my commandments, you will abide in my love, even as I have kept my Father's commandments and abide in His love. I have spoken these things to you that my joy may be in you and that your joy may be full. This is my commandment: That you love one another just as I have loved you."

Love is the key to healing mankind and nature. The law of equality is one of the keys to living the law of love. Let us replace thoughts and feelings of superiority and inferiority with those of divine equality. Let us envision all of mankind following spiritual laws just as God does and wills for us to do. By so doing, our joy and the joy of every living being in this world will be full. For God blesses us all—equally.

GIVE & TAKE

An Old Testament proverb states, "The wise in heart will take commandments." Taking, as with all other activities, comes under divine jurisdiction. It is one half of one cosmic law, a commandment of our Father-Mother God: to give and to take.

At first glance, this looks like an easy law to comprehend; so much so, that we may tend to pass it by in our thoughts without dwelling on it long enough to appreciate fully how powerful, how critical and how tremendously vast is this law that shapes our world. For example, take us as spiritual beings in our physical relationship with the elements of Earth. On June 27, 1966, my high Self, Nada, channeled this information about give-and-take in our love exchange with another kingdom:

"We . . . may extend our premise to the love principle within the elemental kingdom and see that these elements, which create our atmosphere and which allow us to have the form in which we are having our experience on this planet during the present time, *give* in love that which we require. They work in sympathy and in harmony with that which they *receive* from the race of man. This particular subject is . . . the highest point of communication in mankind on the third dimensional level while he is in a physical body. Until he can appreciate and learn this power of communicating love and receiving love from the elements, he will suffer many strange and severe conditions as far as weather and atmosphere are concerned."

In this case, communicating love means giving love, and receiving love is the same as taking love. The communication indicates how critical the law of give-and-take is in fulfilling the law of love, no matter with whom or with what we are interacting. Just look at the current desecration of the temple we call planet Earth. It shows that man does not know fully how to love until he knows how to give and how to take.

Before we concern ourselves with how we should give and take, let's look at one example of this law in nature: *symbiosis*. It is a biological term for the living together of two dissimilar organisms because it is advantageous to both. One of the most spectacular and far-reaching examples of this is the 300-million-year-old symbiotic relationship between fungi and plants. Known as mycorrhizal association, symbiotic fungi associate with the roots of plants. They are responsible for helping plants rapidly take in nutrients, such as nitrates and phosphates. In return, plants are thought to exude or make available through their roots organic compounds like sugars, which benefit the fungi.

According to Lynn Margulis and Karlene Schwartz, in *Five Kingdoms: An Illustrated Guide to the Phyla of Life on Earth,* nearly all healthy terrestrial plants, with the exception of mosses and moss allies, have symbiotic fungi with their roots. The law of give-and-take in just this one form contributes to the health of virtually all land plants on Earth. We would do well to thank and to love these species of the much-maligned Kingdom Fungi, not only for the well-being of land plants, but also for their positive effects on all the plants that provide food, shelter and so forth for the higher orders of life, such as animals and man.

Margulis and Schwartz further report that some scientists, on the basis of increasing evidence, are now hypothesizing that this give-and-take mycorrhizal association was "a prerequisite to the coming ashore of all the land plants," all of which have a common ancestry in aquatic green algae of the Kingdom Protoctista. It is stunning to think of how critical and influential this law may have been in the evolution of life on Earth.

What are some of the key elements of this important law? The law is give-and-take. It is one law. There is no law of giving. Neither is there a law of receiving. There is only the law of give-and-take; two polar aspects of one single procedure. It is similar to our Father-Mother God being one God and not two Gods, or our conscious and subconscious representing two aspects of one mind and not two minds. An act of giving is incomplete without at some point taking or receiving something in return. Likewise, an act of taking is incomplete without giving something back.

To which should we give more emphasis, giving or taking? Neither. We need to concentrate on both equally. If we devote our energy to giving and giving and giving and refuse to receive anything in return, the exchange becomes imbalanced. In the extreme case, this leads to various kinds of martyrdom. By the law of give-and-take, any idea we might have that, in order to fulfill spiritual laws, God would make us overextend our giving to the point of imbalancing our minds or emotions, or of impairing our health, is neither just nor true. And it never will be.

On the other hand, if we spend all of our time taking and taking and taking, without giving in return, we become parasites. No living being is supposed to live at the expense of another, thinking or acting as if he/she/it can thrive on the works or the energies of another without compensation. For compensation is a divine law.

After preparing his twelve disciples, Jesus sent them out to spread the good news. "Freely you have received, freely give," he instructed them. In a channeling on July 16, 1966, Sananda-Jesus elaborated on this statement: "The law of divine truth is that you shall give what you receive; and then you shall receive even greater, after having given that which was given first unto you in the name of goodness, in the name of truth, in the name of love."

God's example is this: give first and receive second. The law is give-and-take, not take-and-give. Yes, we first have taken from God. But that doesn't mean we are to take first from others. In order to live up to our I Am nature, to act in God's image and likeness, we need to give first, like God. Then we will receive as God receives. Spirit receives from us when we give to others. We receive from Spirit through the love of others for us after we have already given.

One of the clearest analyses of giving is recorded in the *Bhagavad Gita*. Basically, there are three levels. *Sattvic* is the most pure and spiritual. *Rajasic* is tainted with selfishness, and *tamasic* is total ignorance about how to give. The *Gita* states: "Giving simply because it is right to give, without thought of return, at a proper time, in proper circumstances, and to a worthy person, is *sattvic* giving. Giving with regrets or in expectation of receiving some favor or of getting something in return is *rajasic*. Giving at an inappropriate time, in inappropriate circumstances, and to an unworthy person, without affection or respect, is *tamasic*."

In giving more consistently and divinely, it helps to remember that when we give to another we are giving to Spirit as well.

How shall we take? One of the main cautions given by spiritual masters throughout history is not to be selfish. Take only what is needed. Gautama Buddha said: "Do not turn away what is given you, nor reach out for what is given to others, lest you disturb your quietness. Give thanks for what has been given you, however little. Be pure, never falter."

Lao Tzu states, "He who knows that enough is enough will always have enough." In the Sermon on the Mount, Jesus teaches us to pray, "Give us today our daily bread." We are to ask Spirit to give us what we need from day to day, not to give us what we need for the rest of our lives right now.

To give and to take acceptably takes a good deal of practice. Perfect giving requires perfect taking. Perfect taking or receiving necessitates perfect giving.

Our exchange with God, mankind and nature can only be as pure as the location of our exchange: our mind, body and soul. This is the temple site wherein all of our commerce is conducted with others and with God.

One of the first things Jesus did upon returning to Jerusalem for the last time was to chase out moneychangers, buyers and sellers who turned the temple of God into an exchange of materialism. Let us now ask Spirit to assist us and the race of man to clear our temple; to clean up the table that is our conscious and subconscious mind, our emotions, and our soul memories, so that we first can receive purely from Spirit.

On our table, let there be bread and wine. The Christ within us says, "Take, eat; this is my body." So let us incorporate *corpus Christi,* the body of Christ, the light body, in our mortal expression. The Christ also says, "Take, drink of it, all of you. This is my blood of the new testament which is shed for many." That is, let our hearts take the laws of life, take God's commandments, take His-Her divine love, so that our giving will be as our Creator's.

God is eternal. Our relationship with Spirit and Its children is eternal. Therefore, let us be wise and take commandments, and let us give, forevermore.

FREE WILL

Two cosmic laws, free will and noninterference, directly apply to freedom. Though they are closely linked, and almost inseparable from one another, they can be isolated in one respect. Free will relates most strongly to personal, internal freedom. Noninterference correlates to external, interpersonal, international, interkingdom, interdimensional freedoms and so on.

A good example of this difference was given by Jesus in a communication on April 4, 1958. He was discussing free will in relation to his crucifixion and how certain factions of Jews thought that the Messiah was to free them from Roman occupiers. Jesus said: "But my mission, like yours, is not to free man from his own bondage, one man's of another, but to free all men from the yoke of physical bondage; to bring him into a higher consciousness in order to raise him closer to God, pure and holy. For you cannot come to God's pure and clear channel if you are impure and bespeckled with Earthly passions and misinterpretation of God's laws and purposes."

One man's bondage of another correlates with the law of noninterference, which we will cover in the next chapter. In this chapter, we are going to deal with that which relates to freeing oneself from physical or mortal bondage: free will.

Free will, according to *Webster's New Universal Unabridged Dictionary,* is "the human will regarded as free from restraints, compulsions, or any antecedent conditions; freedom of decision or choice." From the point of view of cosmic law, this definition is only half correct, and therefore it is not surprising that there is continuing confusion over free will, even to the point where some question whether free will does, in fact, exist. This is what Jesus referred to in the communication when he said that we cannot come closer to God when we continue to misinterpret God's laws. So, let us analyze this definition point by point.

The statement that free will is "the human will regarded as free from restraints" is incorrect. Free will is derived from Spirit's will. Spirit's will comprises at least twenty-three universal principles; and even Spirit must follow every one of them.

In a channeled communication on April 24, 1958, Jesus said: "When the Father gave His Christ children the freedom of choice known as free will, He had to consider that His children could choose other satisfactions in His creation to the one and only permanent satisfaction: remaining pure in spirit. The Father could make no conditions in His gift of free will. His laws are unchangeable, even for Himself. He must first obey the law, to be the law. So must you obey His laws before you can be with Him in eternal life, enjoying His grace and His glory."

If even Spirit is restricted in Its use of free will, how is it possible that man is not? The restriction God has placed on free will is that all other cosmic principles act in concert with it. This divine formulation precludes human will as free from restraint.

This part of man's loose definition of free will has led to immoral acts and institutions throughout history, some of which continue to this day. It also has caused many to resist the concept of a higher power, of a divine order, of God. For many, believing in the existence of a greater, divine will and power threatens their concept of personal freedom or takes it away altogether. If there are divine laws that maintain cosmic balance and harmony and if there is an omnipotent and omniscient God, of what use are one person's decisions and efforts? What possible purpose can there be for personal free will, anyway?

This line of reasoning is one explanation for why people and whole societies, such as pre-Islamic Arabia and China during the Shang Dynasty, as well as some in the present day and age, adopt fatalistic thinking. This kind of thinking says, "Well, it happened, so I guess it was meant to be," or "Whatever happens must be the will of God or the will of the gods."

On March 28, 1958, Paul the Apostle communicated: "Nothing is ever so clearly defined that you cannot change it, possibly by other thoughts, other actions than anticipated, according to the road and the pattern you have developed. Nothing is solid and firmly planned in the entire universe. There is a fluidity and a freedom which is based on the principle of free will. All creatures, including man, have this freedom of will. The birds, the beasts, the plant realms have free will as you, mankind, have free will. Nothing is forced. Force is a stagnant condition; a solid, immovable mass of void. The universe, and all that is created in it, is fluid and free to compass its own future."

We need not fear losing our freedom to think, feel and act. There is no power on Earth nor in heaven that will separate Spirit's law of free will from our being. Our free will is a necessary ingredient of divine order. It is eternally secure, and can never be separated from God's will.

Another statement in the dictionary definition was that free will is "the human will regarded as free from . . . any antecedent [preceding] conditions." But this too is inadequate. Only societies with an imperfect understanding of other divine laws, such as cause and effect (karma) and reincarnation, could conceive of true freedom without incorporating past actions as present obligations. Who can wonder why man would have a pattern of evading responsibility for his own actions, or of not feeling obligated to compensate for others' lack of responsibility, if free will means that what has been done in the past is of no account?

The apostle Paul wrote, "Whatever a man sows, that shall he also reap." In the Buddhist scripture, the *Dhammapada,* the Buddha instructs: "Those who are selfish suffer here and hereafter; they suffer in both worlds from the results of their own actions. But those who are selfless rejoice here and rejoice hereafter. They rejoice in both worlds from the results of their own actions."

In Christianity the laws of free will and cause and effect are expressed accurately, limited only by Christianity's nonrecognition of the law of reincarnation. All of the major Asian religions—Jainism, Brahmanism, Hinduism, Sikhism, the Parsi sect, and Buddhism—embrace free will, karma *and* reincarnation. In these religions the idea of freedom within the parameters of past actions is well developed. However, the goal of life is perceived to be freedom from karma, a cosmic law, and freedom from the need for reincarnation, which is another cosmic law.

But karma and reincarnation, even when they involve past errors, are not activities to be freed from. We must use them in conjunction with all the other cosmic laws, in order to achieve true freedom. We can never separate ourselves from these principles, any more than we can separate ourselves from God. We will always be causing effects and reincarnating, if not here on Earth then somewhere else. To fulfill obligations and redress negative, antecedent conditions by our I Am Self-directed freewill choice is a necessary and good spiritual activity. Compliance with any divine law requires exertion of our free will.

Man's definition of free will is true in that it means "freedom of decision or choice," and it also means that to have it, we must be "free from . . . compulsions." God gave us free will. As much as Divine Mind guides and influences us through our Christ Self, we never have been nor ever will be compelled or coerced to follow divine will.

In a communication on September 13, 1961, Sananda revealed that within each of us Spirit as divine will is perfect: "There are two wills in man: the will of the self—the lower self, the mortal self—and the will of Spirit within, which is always perfect and intuned. Free will is the will of God to give you your choice. For you would not be a true agent, a true child of God . . . without your own will to use, to command and to utilize for good. . . .

"You have built up, through many incarnations, a desire pattern, or an understanding or an evolution, of will. But always the divine will is perfect, and is ready to serve and to be done. It is up to you to discriminate, to find the difference within yourself when divine will [I Am Self] speaks and when [mortal] self will speaks. It is then up to you to choose between these two. Then it is up to you to use the power justly, wisely and completely!"

What, then, compels us, of our own free will, to depart from divine will? Every religion has its list: anger, jealousy, lust, greed, cultural and peer pressures, selfishness, attachment, idolatry and the like. True spiritual masters will guide others, by what theologians call voluntary necessity, to deal with these compulsions. *Voluntary necessity* means that the master says what must necessarily be done for a person's salvation or transcendence while, at the same time, he or she does not interfere with the person's free will. In this way the person's actions remain strictly voluntary.

A perfect example of this is the last part of Moses' farewell address to the Israelites before they entered the Promised Land: "This commandment which I command you this day is not hidden from you, neither is it far off. It is not in heaven, that you should say, Who shall go up for us to heaven and bring it to us, that we may hear it and do it? . . . But the word is very near you, in your mouth and in your heart, that you may do it.

"See, I have set before you this day life and good, and death and misfortunes; in that I command you this day to love the Lord your God, to walk in His ways, and to keep His commandments and His statutes and His judgments; then you shall live. . . . Therefore choose life."

We are in the Latter Days preceding, not a promised land, but a promised consciousness: the second coming of our own Christ consciousness and the Second Coming of the leader of this planet, Sananda-Jesus, in the next few decades. Let us close with one further example of voluntary necessity and of guidance about free will, from the highest spiritual authority in this solar system, Archangel Michael, who addresses all humanity on Earth. Delivered on August 17, 1966, it is, in cosmic time cycles, as much a closing address before the Second Coming as Moses' address was for the Israelites long ago.

"Choose ye now what you will serve. For this is the day of accounting, this is the time, now is the hour. . . . Should the soul then choose to become part of this evolutionary growth pattern, change and transmutation, you will remain here and will experience as much of this development as you desire to participate in and with. Should the conscious will or mortal personality desire to have other experiences or not accept what is here presented, you will be respected. For all men are given free will; and this is never declined or taken away, but given to its last full measure everywhere that there are life and freedom.

"Be then where you wish to be. Do then what you wish to do. But ask first, is it your mortal wish or your spiritual wish? Adhere to it and do that which you are given to do. Change that which you are given to change. Develop those talents which you are given to develop. Become that which is inherent in you: the God Self, the Christ potential, the life force of Spirit."

NONINTERFERENCE

Let us delve into a great mystery, one that is of vital concern to all who are trying to lead decent lives and fulfill the purposes of their incarnations. Why do "bad" things happen? Why does God allow them to happen? Our focus is the divine law of noninterference.

In these present turbulent times and throughout history, it has been very difficult for anyone to live on Earth and remain true to his highest nature, the Christ Self, accomplishing his soul mission without incurring negative karma. Negative karma is action that causes effects that will require more time and energy and, oftentimes, more lifetimes in the future to balance or cancel out and leave the doer free of debt.

Christ Jesus' instruction to his disciples was to be in the world but not of it. Creating karmic relationships that require further lessons is one of the ways we become "of the world."

For centuries before Jesus' life, students and disciples in the Indian subcontinent were hearing a similar instruction from their teachers. Recorded in the oldest known religious texts in existence, Hinduism's Vedas, it is repeated in the Upanishads: "Two birds, fair of plumage, close in friendship, cling to the selfsame tree. One of this pair eats its sweet berry; not partaking, the other gazes on." According to Michael Nagler, Associate Professor of Classics and Comparative Literature at the University of California, Berkeley, the correct model for life was interpreted to be the latter: "He or she who is not pulled into the stream of phenomena achieves the supreme human destiny."

By our understanding of the proper expression of the law of noninterference, we can become more efficient stewards of the energy and life of our Father-Mother God that flows through us. Our brothers and sisters on the higher planes of evolvement, who are helping us, fully appreciate this law, as Wains explained in a communication on May 18, 1960:

"There shall not be another global war on this planet without intervention by space visitors, who wish not to interfere; and cannot interfere without uniting with your karmic matters. This is serious business on any level. But we repeat: no global war shall be permitted without last resorts. Last resorts for any highly developed understanding being is undertaking karmic unity with you and your free will. We are your brothers in love. Love is the key. We are your brothers to teach, to educate you in ways of God's divine law, love. Can love be any clearer?"

One of the ultimate acts of love is overriding the free will of another for his or her own good and for the good of all concerned. This is done with extreme caution and only for the right reasons, as in those cases to prevent harm or injury to someone. Meddling with a person's free will is a last resort. So, this message gives us important information about the truth and the karmic consequences of the law of noninterference.

Noninterference is a spiritual principle that prohibits intruding into the affairs of others without invitation or justification. This law is strongly bound up with the law of free will. Whereas free will allows personal freedom of choice, or internal freedoms, noninterference allows for external freedom between life forms: between people, between people and all other organisms in nature, and between a person and God. By the law of noninterference, we simply cannot intervene in the concerns of others without some continued karmic obligation if they do not give their consent. In some cases, this is why our prayers are not answered.

Have you ever asked yourself the question, "Why is this happening to me?" You are not alone. According to a 1986 Lutheran survey of twenty-four pastors in seventeen states in the United States, and a subsequent informal survey of South Florida clergy of many different faiths and denominations by the *Miami Herald* in August of that year, it is the question most asked of clergy by their members.

Those with a deep understanding of God, of His laws, assume responsibility in some way for the situations they find themselves in. If those situations are negative, they work in positive ways and know that some good will come out of them, that some lesson will be learned. Unfortunately, many people in the survey also phrase the question, "Why is God causing this bad thing to happen? Why is He letting it happen?"

It is not divine will that causes bad things to happen, but man's will, when he is ignorant of cosmic laws and lacks the love and desire to live by them. So, the real question is: when is it divine will to let "bad" things happen? Rephrased: when does divine wisdom allow lessons to be learned the hard way?

On January 30, 1963, Sol-O-Man, who was Mary, mother of Jesus, channeled this answer: "God is good. Therefore, that which is good is love, and love is good for all things equally. When it behooves the love principle of God to allow error to exist in one of Its creations or the children of man, It expects this to be unfolded fully in order that the lesson be painfully sharp and clear unto the incarnational pattern of the souls who bring it about by malevolent influences around them and in themselves. Only by cleansing and clearing this through the scrubbing process and the agonizing process of purging can you be sure that it will be removed, is removed and never can return. . . .

"I tell you that only in love and with love can you express the will of almighty good, which is God. I tell you that this is the duty and the privilege of each and every soul incarnated: to bring about his own fulfillment of Christ in action through his personal development or individualization."

Many times Divine Mind, our high Self or our spiritual teachers will not intervene on our behalf out of love. They know that we have an opportunity of exercising greater divine will, and of developing a stronger desire to enact it. They know they would be interfering with many divine laws by not allowing us, on our own, to learn better use of free will, transmutation, cause and effect, and other laws.

Such is the way of love, the greatest law for us to learn on Earth. In one case, spiritual forces will intervene on our behalf; in another case, they will allow errors to occur. What are we to do? How are we correctly to discern and to utilize this law of noninterference? Are we to intervene? What parent would allow her child to run out into a street full of traffic? When are we to stand aside and let friends we love settle their differences without our help? As for the environment, should we let nature take its course, or should we interact to help balance it?

In an interview by the *Washington Post* in the spring of 1987, Thomas Lovejoy, then vice-president of the World Wildlife Fund, said that man must take action to conserve nature. In the early 1960s, the United States Park Service had a hands-off policy of nonintervention, allowing nature to manage its own affairs. This philosophy is described in the Taoist scripture, the *Tao te ching:* "The world is ruled by letting things take their course. It cannot be ruled by interfering."

However, this kind of management, which Lovejoy labeled "management by neglect," will not work now that man's environmental destruction threatens this planet's ability to sustain life. He said, "We simply have to learn how to intervene properly, and to manage it positively."

This is what Taoism calls Primal Virtue. The *Tao te ching* says, "Creating without claiming, doing without taking credit, guiding without interfering, this is Primal Virtue."

The task before humankind is to spiritualize life on this planet without interfering. How do we promote harmonious human interactions on all levels with one another, with plants, animals, minerals, God and family, nations and cultures, without unwanted and, by the law of noninterference, unauthorized intervention in another's free will?

We each must find the answer for ourselves, case by case. The answer for one situation, person or time may not satisfy the needs of another. Making mistakes is a normal part of our spiritual growth in mastering this, a most difficult, spiritual law.

This law does not mean that we should withdraw from interacting with the rest of life. On the contrary, the most enlightened spiritual teachers of every age challenge humankind to have loving and harmonious relations with every living being, since we all participate in the divine oneness. As it is written in the Hindu scripture, the *Bhagavad Gita,* "Every selfless act . . . is born from Brahman, the eternal, infinite Godhead. He is present in every act of service. All life turns on this law. . . . Whoever violates it, indulging his senses for his own pleasure and ignoring the needs of others, has wasted his life. . . . Strive constantly to serve the welfare of the world; by devotion to selfless work one attains the supreme goal of life."

Serving the welfare of the world through love is the supreme goal of life. All of us should participate in life and love to the fullest.

We should ask for help and assistance for whatever we truly need. In asking, we, of our own free will, open the door to exchange, cooperation and communication with Spirit and with others. Everyone can then help and serve one another without violating the law of noninterference.

All of this requires the light of understanding, which is another element of the divine trinity of life, light and love. Light refers to enlightenment, knowledge and wisdom. It is said that knowing others is wisdom but knowing oneself is enlightenment. Let us ask for enlightenment. Let us find out from the I Am Self what we can know about ourselves that will amplify the light in us, so that we can emanate that light and amplify the light, life and love in others.

We ask that the law of noninterference be fulfilled by all in all interactions as of now, the eternal present. So be it.

ORDER

Virtually every creation myth ever recorded describes supernatural forces or a Supreme Being fashioning order out of chaos. Since prehistory, man has held order as an ideal of the first rank. Today, only one religious/philosophical system in the world glorifies chaos. All others affirm a belief in supreme, universal laws governing all celestial and terrestrial phenomena. Like many other cultures and civilizations, the ancient Greeks created a word for world and universal order: *kosmos* ("cosmos").

Order as a cosmic, divine law refers to the observance of laws; to regular, sequential and periodic arrangements of things and events. Assigned the "law of arrangement" in the dictionary, *order* also is defined as systems and methods subject to rules and laws. Divine order implies that Spirit's perfectly created and properly arranged eternal patterns are upheld by divine principles and procedures. Therefore, it is incumbent upon all sentient beings to become aware

71

of and to follow divine laws and methods which uphold Spirit's original order.

In terms of physical existence and worldly dealings, the law of order is ubiquitous. Everything having to do with systems, patterns, models, regularity, periodicity, frequency, series, lists, matrices and cycles has order as its ruling principle. Various systems that support business, management, communications, economics, education, and scientific investigation, to name a few, reflect the powerful impact the divine law of order exerts on modern civilization.

Order in the natural world can be observed in magnificent diversity: the procession of daily and seasonal cycles of sun, moon, stars and tides; life cycles; biochemical cycles; the rhythm of breathing and heartbeat; skeletal, nervous, circulatory and other physiological systems; electromagnetic energy oscillation; the periodic table of the elements; the orderly internal arrangement of atoms in minerals; time scales; color scales; musical scales, and the energy spectrum. The list is endless.

Since time immemorial, man's response to natural order has been to emulate this principle in his laws, religious rites, belief systems, scientific methods and philosophic approaches. In his overview on law and religion in *The Encyclopedia of Religion,* Harold Berman writes: "In virtually all societies the established legal processes of allocating rights and duties, resolving conflicts, and creating channels of cooperation are inevitably connected with the community's sense of, and commitment to, ultimate values and purposes."

Among many notable examples, Berman cites Hebrew, Muslim and Hindu legal systems. Because Hebrew and Muslim systems of law are based on the prophetic revelation of God's higher laws, the observance of civil law in their civilizations was regarded as a religious act. God gave divine laws as a blueprint or pattern for man to follow. Therefore, obedience to law was not only a personal concern but a national obligation.

In the classical Hindu legal system, law and religion are inseparable in the concept of dharma. *Dharma* comes from the Sanskrit *dhri,* which literally means "to support." Dharma embodies divine laws, and these support the order of natural laws and life on Earth. Individuals and rulers alike have a unique personal dharma which they are obliged to fulfill to support the moral and universal order.

The lawful obligation or dharma of a ruler was to make sure that all citizens he governed succeeded in expressing their dharma. If a law was broken, punishment and penance were prescribed not merely to compensate for material injury, damages or losses. The primary object was to regain the moral and divine order of the universe. Israelite laws were similarly perceived as active forms of behavior that preserved God's order and will rather than as passive, punitive measures to redress legal-code violations. In both these cases, the foremost priority was the dual rehabilitation of the person and of the cosmic order.

Rehabilitation should be the top priority of every legal system on this planet today. Since man's fall from grace, Spirit in essence has been rehabilitating us back into our true, inherent spiritual being. Eternal punishment or damnation is a false, man-made concept. God heals infractions of divine law, departures from the cosmic order, by love. Every person is an integral part of the cosmos. Each one's God-given, unique contribution of love and service is required to uphold the order of the universe. As long as even one member of the family of man is unable to give that love, there cannot be perfect order.

In a February 6, 1963, communication, the apostle Paul channeled information about divine laws, order, and their relationship to God. Paul, known as Hilarion on the etheric planes, is a member of the Hierarchal Board, the spiritual government of ascended masters whose obligation is to maintain divine order in this solar system.

"We do not proffer to you one system, but we offer multitudinous systems that have been used on every form and every level of creation where there are form and intelligent life. Do not think for one minute that all intelligent life is as man sees it; in other words, a man form, with animal and vegetable kingdoms.

"There are intelligent forms of life which have ways of systems, governments and societies that are unlike those which are found in our present solar system. . . . But in these forms and in these organizations they follow the same divine principles that are, and must be, always. For God is the rules or the regulations of divine procedure.

"The word *God* is a simplified terminology meaning divine law, good, order. Use those words and those letters alone. Often it is told that God symbolizes all that is good. This is true. But good is what is the fundamental law that is unchangeable. This is what is good. It also is divine, in the fact that it cannot be changed regardless of the formation it takes. Therefore, if you are to follow this principle and to bring about goodness and God's divine plan, you must follow the laws that are unchangeable. Integration, unity, relationship and interdependence, one form with another, are part of this goodness, this order, this divinity which is God. . . .

"There are many gospels, there are many books and there are many scriptures that have come down through the ages, and all speak the same fundamental law: integration, unity, oneness, love.

"These are the divine laws of the universe; that no matter what form it has taken, no matter what experiment or experience it desires, it feels its way through these fundamental first orders. There are second and third levels of orders which are in the form of experimentation; but the first orders or the first rules of the Divine are unchangeable and must be adhered to regardless of the realm, the dimension or the creation."

This book attempts to summarize the universal, first-order laws of the cosmos. It would be impossible to cover all of the divine patterns and procedures on display throughout God's creation. However, we can mention a few of the ways Spirit Itself is organized.

Besides cosmic laws, the Godhead manifests seven divine attributes known as the Seven Rays or Flames of Life. At the head of each of the seven rays is a being, an elohim, who represents and expresses that ray. On March 19, 1969, in a communication on the hierarchal order of the creation and evolution of man, Sananda-Jesus shed light on the existence and functioning of the Seven Rays of Life:

"Beyond the angelic realm are the Seven Flames of Life or elohim, the lights or the light of God seven times manifested, each giving expression to one or more aspects of the God Force.

"In this rhythm and change of mastership and chain of command we begin, in all evolution, with the elohim; who speak the word, who hold the force, who are part of the Godhead, the magnificent Mother-Father Divine Self radiation. This is unmanifested glory and the opposite polarities and perfect balance and perfect expression of impulse by which each thing is derived.

"Seven steps are required to bring about manifested form. Seven words or ideas are involved. . . . Out of the Godhead come the initial seven; who are part of God, but not all of God: will and power, intelligence and wisdom, love and feeling, cohesion or crystallization, healing or balance, cleansing and purification, rest and peace finalized. . . .

"It begins on the realms and in the consciousness of those that are the elohim, out of the Godhead. It is entrusted into the hands of the angelic, celestial planes, whereby all the elements are in divine control and creative force. It is held under the guardianship of the celestial realm until the special creation of God, the Son, the race of man, can comprehend that service or area of performance. Under the sons of God all lesser forms of creation which are in the process of evolution, the animal and the vegetable and the mineral kingdoms, are held in balance and in supervision. . . .

"Whereby each man, who is a spiritual son of the Godhead, is created out of the word of one of the seven aspects, he must serve upon that aspect or flame. You call them rays of life. When a son or individuality is created under the auspices of the elohim, any one of these flames, you are eternally pledged unto that source and under that supervision. You may not be removed from that, for that is your God Self or the spark of life from out of that particular flame or ray of life. . . .

"You may be very much aware of and you may be consciously functioning under one ray that is your proper fundamental home source or base. Yet you must always pay homage to and have a certain amount of experience with every other one of the seven rays in operation. These flames of life are as essential to your existence as your realization as a spiritual being, a son, a part of God."

The true concept of Spirit's Divine Trinity, which finds its expression in many religions and philosophies, was succinctly presented by Paul the Apostle in a communication on March 13, 1958:

"God is a dual force, negative and positive. When this pole reproduces a creative field It creates only love; the energy, the emotion, the constructive force in nature which is known as love or Christ. Christ therefore is the only true begotten Son of God the Father and God the Mother. In each one of God's children is implanted this creative force, the Christ consciousness. In each one of us is God's light. In this way every creature is God's only begotten Son. That is the essence and the meaning of the Holy Trinity."

Since ancient times, cultures worldwide have produced rites of initiation which offer an ordered method to transcend mortal life and achieve immortal life. The seven major initiations to attain Christ consciousness, the source of inspiration for all spiritual initiations, were revealed by my high Self, Nada, in a channeling on April 7, 1969:

"There are seven basic initiations the Christed soul must accept and pass through in order to have the full demonstration of . . . Christed illumination for the planet and all life form upon it. . . . These initiations are steps or avenues of development created by the Spirit within in order to assure that spiritual Self for the ongoing and the trust with which the individual soul may meet and work. Never does Spirit give more than the individual soul or the individual body form can accept and handle. Therefore, when Spirit prepares these steps of initiation, . . . you have to understand they are for your highest good and set there in order for you to determine your own place and your own strength and your own future. . . .

"The first step is the spiritual awakening or the *birth* of spiritual consciousness. This is the birth of the Christ. . . . The second step is the initiation of the *baptism*. This takes place within every individual when the fire of the Spirit descends upon the consciousness, and all that you are and all that you wish to become is bathing your entire auric field. You become immersed in this energy and this fire. Fire and water together are a symbol here, used as counterbalances so you will understand that the fire of Spirit cannot be put out by the waters of your own immersing or bathing or cleansing.

"There is a dual aspect in this baptism. For you feel the energy of fire coursing through your entire body and mind and you feel aflame with all the power God has given each of His-Her individual creations, His-Her own sons, which you are. Then you feel the desire to bathe yourself for cleanliness. You feel the desire to disperse any of the errors of your ways and all the evil that may have been done in your life. . . .

"The third step is that when the feeling nature and the love *transmutation* start to take place. This is when the individual begins to realize he is all love, and that love can be directed and can cause the change within his own beingness. This is the beginning of changing the self from man into spirit, I Am. . . .

"The fourth step is known as *transfusion*. This is the point where the individual is so infused with the spiritual consciousness and the I Am Self from within his pattern that he begins to understand his place upon the planet and his works that are required unto him. . . . It is in this fourth step that man begins to know who he is and why he has come to the place where he has arrived. . . .

"As we move into the fifth step or initiation, . . . we understand it from this point of view: the *transfiguration* is possible only because the doorway between dimensions is fully opened. . . . At the epitome of the transfiguration step or the fifth initiation we know then that the doorway is totally opened, totally controlled and the individual can step back and forth into any of the other dimensions. . . . He can have transfigured over himself, totally transforming him, those who are working with him and those expressions of his own past lives that he has experienced which have led him to the present step or level or life incarnation where he is at that time.

"The sixth initiation is that which has to do primarily with the pineal gland. This is the *crucifixion* and the *resurrection.* . . . The initiation or the sixth step that man must perform is the resurrection after the crucifixion. So we always combine these two as one. This step of crucifixion–resurrection must be demonstrated over a period of time. . . . It brings about not only a descent of Spirit into the mind and into the function of the brain, which controls the body and thereby transforms it totally from a third into a fourth dimensional vehicle, but it brings about a totally new level of understanding and works. . . .

"The *ascension,* which is the seventh and final demonstration by a Christed being, means the ability to take the life energy and the form that has been resurrected into the next dimension. It means the body that has been resurrected, the mind or consciousness which has remained clear and open and unbroken, can be moved by the power that is within the individual at that time into the next sphere of works."

When followed, all of these divine manifestations of the spiritual principle of order–cosmic laws, the Seven Rays of Life, the Holy Trinity, the seven spiritual initiations–ensure that all fulfill their dharma which supports the divine order of the cosmos. For what purpose does divine order support all of this magnificent, unfathomable life on Earth? *For love, always for love!*

CAUSE & EFFECT

Cause and effect is one of the great laws of the universe. The significance of this law, unlike other divine statutes, is that its manifestation in the world and throughout the cosmos is not diminished by man's misuse or nonuse.

Whether humankind works with this law for good or willfully resists this law, every thought, emotion and action creates an effect, positive or negative. Even neutral thoughts (ambivalence), apathetic emotions, and inactions (sins of omission) have consequences, or produce effects after their kind. Those effects will determine other causes and other effects one after the other into infinity. Only by working with this law positively will our dharma, that is to say, our personal obligation to uphold the divine order of the universe, be fulfilled. This grand and awesome principle must be given its due if true happiness and wholesome living are to be attained.

The law of cause and effect also is known as karma. For many in the West, karma only implies former actions that lead to present situations or future conditions. But the true definition of karma encompasses both past and present actions and their results.

Karma literally means "something done"; it comes from the Sanskrit root *kri,* meaning "to do." Karma combines present actions with influential past actions. Karmic memories as received via our subconscious could be memories of good or bad experiences of this or former incarnations. They also may include remembrances of our eternal Christ nature and light-body experiences. Memories of high Self demonstrations are always good and positively guide our lives.

Because karma is one of God's divine laws that serves a divine purpose, it should not be thought of only as a form of bondage or as something totally negative from which one seeks to be released, as some Eastern philosophies espouse. For there is such a thing as positive karma.

In a channeled question-and-answer session on October 25, 1960, Jesus relayed this information on cause and effect: "The law of the universe is scientific. The law of the universe is what all science tries to discover. . . . The basic law of the universe is cause and effect: what you sow, you shall reap. Men have mistaken it. Only in the spiritual sense have they interpreted, and left it to religions. In some cases they have discovered this law in their physical sciences.

"However, it is true in every realm in every way. As soon as man learns this unbreakable law, he evolves to the next higher step in evolution. It is through this understanding that he stops making mistakes, because then he knows he must reap that error if he plants it. Then he begins to plant only good so he can reap only good.

"This is what Moses brought. This is what Buddha and Krishna and every great teacher brought to man. This is what I, Jesus of Nazareth, brought. Man has ignored it. But you cannot separate science from this divine law. It is one and the same."

Isaac Newton, born in 1642 in England, is widely regarded as the greatest scientist of all time. One of his works, *Principia,* is considered the greatest scientific work ever written. Rather less well known is that he wrote far more about theological and alchemical matters than about mathematics and physics.

The law of physics that most directly describes the law of cause and effect is Newton's third law of motion. In short, it says that for every action there is an equal and opposite reaction. Newton called the two phases of the law's single force, action and reaction forces. He also understood that, in terms of physical matter, it was impossible to have one without the other and that either force could equally be called active or reactive.

The only scientist to refine and add to this law appreciably was Albert Einstein. The originator of the theory of relativity, he is regarded as the greatest scientist in modern times. In *Ideas and Opinions,* a book of his collected writings, Einstein wrote:

"You will hardly find one among the profounder sort of scientific minds without a religious feeling of his own. . . . The scientist is possessed by the sense of universal causation. The future, to him, is every whit as necessary and determined [determined in the sense of having an exact reason or cause] as the past. . . . His religious feeling takes the form of a rapturous amazement at the harmony of natural law, which reveals an intelligence of such superiority that, compared with it, all the systematic thinking and acting of human beings is an utterly insignificant reflection."

Positivism, materialism and scientism, known also as reductionism and physicalism, are philosophical systems that use the findings of physical science as the only true source of information to explain reality. These philosophies and science, therefore, are limited to what and how much matter and energy can be measured by present technology. In these approaches, causation and its effects are confined to physical, material reality.

The great religions and metaphysicians throughout history have contributed to our knowledge of the law of cause and effect by showing how this law works in the presently immeasurable thought realms. In the first chapter of the *Dhammapada,* which means "path of dharma" or "path of divine order," the Buddha says, "Our life is shaped by our mind; we become what we think."

The tenth commandment revealed to Moses is not to covet, not to envy that which is not rightfully ours. Coveting is not a physical act. It is an intention, a mental and emotional activity which causes bad effects.

During the Sermon on the Mount, Jesus said of the seventh commandment, "Anyone who looks at a woman lustfully has already committed adultery with her in his heart." To emphasize this point, he next referred to the tenth law, saying, "If your right eye should cause you to stumble, pluck it out." This is an Aramaic idiom that means to stop envying. By saying these things, Jesus revealed that all of the laws of Moses which were thought to pertain only to physical acts—murder, adultery, theft, lying—were equally valid prohibitory laws in the unseen realm of thoughts and emotions.

Not only does the law of cause and effect work on every level of our being—physical, emotional, soul, mental and spiritual—it also works directly and indirectly. Jesus said, "If you forgive men their faults, your Father in heaven will also forgive you. But if you do not forgive men, neither will your Father forgive even your faults." He also said, "Every good tree bears good fruit; but a bad tree bears bad fruit. A good tree cannot bear bad fruit, neither can a bad tree bear good fruit." These statements describe how cause and effect works directly.

Sananda-Jesus speaks of the indirect workings of karma in this channeling of February 6, 1974: "If one fails in any degree to live up to his greatest expectations, that is, the I Am consciousness . . . then all who are involved with the individual, seen or unseen, present or not present, are going to suffer diametrically. That means on a bias. It is part of the law of cause and effect which eventually you will learn. It is not in direct opposition that you suffer, but in a bias or perpendicular manner. All karma is diametrically opposed or in a bias to that which appears to be the condition. . . ."

"You wish to relate things in a one-to-one basis: an eye for an eye, a tooth for a tooth. . . . Karma does not work in that mathematical manner, but in this diametrically biased manner."

Remember, we are one race of mankind. Not only do we evolve individually and contend with our own karma, but we evolve collectively in groups and in societies. Therefore, we must contend with the consequences of group or race karma.

There is a common saying in the Consciousness-Only School of Buddhism that "a seed produces a manifestation; a manifestation perfumes a seed; the three elements (seed, manifestation, and perfuming) turn on and on; the cause and effect occur at one and the same time." As with Newton's description, this saying holds that the interplaying forces in cause and effect are unified. Again, it affirms one law. Straightforward actions and reactions are ever "perfumed" by indirect karma–our own or others', from the past or present, either good or bad–which influences everyday decisions and responses.

This cosmic law has another aspect to it. As far as I know, this has not been introduced into man's collective consciousness by any religion or philosophy, major or minor. On August 13, 1963, Glo-Ria channeled: "Nothing is spared from the divine laws of cause and effect. When Moses said 'an eye for an eye' he did not mean it literally in that sense of what it has been taken to mean, although it works as finely as that. . . .

"If you have transgressed in some degree while on Earth and it is not likely that you can gain the best lesson in Earth frequency or astral vibration to remedy that situation, a life sojourn on another planet, even in a more harmonious and happy circumstance, is allotted to you, provided it is felt by Spirit within you that the lesson will be well learned. It does not mean that for every transgression you must suffer mortal burnings and hatreds and feelings of remorse, regret and guilt. It does mean, however, that the lesson must be learned or realized.

"Sometimes you will be taken into another planet of a higher frequency and evolvement in order to teach the very lessons that you missed while you were on Earth. This way you are evolving back and forth, sometimes as a teacher, sometimes as a student, sometimes as a leader, sometimes as a follower. Never forget for one moment that you are Christ in action, you are the Son of God, you are Spirit in motion, you are divinely inherited with power, understanding, love and infinite knowledge.

"When you have taken on a form, regardless of what vibration it may be, but let us say on an Earth vibration, and transgressed the natural laws and thereby set up an effect for yourself that must be corrected, it does not necessarily mean that you will return to the same place and go through the exact experience or a similar experience in order to learn that lesson. You are perfectly capable of going back into the Christ consciousness, projecting a form on another planet, and having to teach the same lesson to someone else whereby, in teaching that lesson, you become quite conscious of how it does affect all life and all form."

Given this information, Jesus' admonition not to judge others becomes keenly significant: "Judge not, that you may not be judged. For with the same judgment that you judge, you will be judged, and with the same measure with which you measure, it will be measured to you."

Rather than harshly judging the faults and errors of others, and thereby perhaps causing one to desire to retaliate or to exact retribution, let us wisely remember the law of love as we live the law of cause and effect. Judgment is best left to Spirit. Our work is to help man's agony come to an end.

As Gautama Buddha said, "For hatred can never put an end to hatred; love alone can. This is an unalterable law. People forget that their lives will end soon. For those who remember, quarrels come to an end."

Let us learn to end our quarrels, so that by our example all of humanity can step into the next higher level of evolution. Let our *cause* always be love, so that our *effect* will always be love.

REINCARNATION

In one of the world's greatest mystical, literary masterpieces, the *Bhagavad Gita,* the mythic personification of divine love within every person, Lord Krishna, speaks to his human charge and student, Arjuna: "You and I have passed through many births, Arjuna. You have forgotten, but I remember them all."

In the West, the cosmic law of reincarnation is commonly associated with Eastern philosophy, and for good reason. The dual concepts of karma (the law of cause and effect) and reincarnation, according to J. Bruce Long in *The Encyclopedia of Religion,* "have done more to shape the whole of Asian thought than any other concept or concepts."

Furthermore, he writes: "It might be difficult to identify an idea or set of ideas that has exercised a comparable influence through the entire scope of Western thought, including the cardinal concepts in the writings of Plato and Aristotle." What is indicated here, beyond the specifics of a single cosmic principle, is the tremendous power that cosmic laws exert within people's minds and lives.

Reincarnation, the doctrine that an individual's soul reappears after death in another and different bodily form, appears early on the scene in human development, much like the law of sacrifice.

For example, the Arunta people of central Australia, whom anthropologists classify as having a Stone Age society, believe in reincarnation. In fact, it is the belief of nonliterate cultures all around the world, leading investigators to conclude that the belief in preexistence and reincarnation arose simultaneously with the birth of human culture.

The great eighteenth-century French philosopher Voltaire proposed: "The doctrine of metempsychosis [reincarnation] is, above all, neither absurd nor useless. . . . It is not more surprising to be born twice than once; everything in nature is resurrection."

However, reincarnation is not taught or believed in the West, particularly in Christian societies, although in the last several decades there have been some signs of change. In a channeled communication on October 4, 1960, Jesus revealed that reincarnation should be taught: "It was never Spirit's will not to teach reincarnation. It is in the teachings. In no religion or in no teachings could it be removed entirely. . . . Always, somehow, somewhere a small seed or spark is left. This is true in Christian and Judaic teachings today. Reincarnation is there, but only in a very small segment of truth. They could not remove it entirely, though many have tried."

One notable example of an early Christian writing that was excluded from the New Testament canon is Luke's *Second Book of Acts.** This book is extraordinary because it shows Mary, mother of Jesus, explaining the law of reincarnation to the apostles and disciples at the time of her ascension. She reviews many of her previous incarnations with Jesus; among them are Jesus' incarnations as Khufu, Melchizedek, Zarathustra, Gautama Buddha and Socrates.

The *Second Book of Acts* originates with the manuscripts of Origen, the greatest Christian theologian of the third century. In a communication through me on March 30, 1964, the apostle Paul gave his authentication to this scripture.

In the gospels of Matthew, Mark and Luke, a "physical" demonstration of the law of reincarnation is described in the accounts of Jesus' transfiguration. This demonstration of Christ consciousness was explained by Archangel Uriel in a communication on August 18, 1970:

"In the transfiguration on the mount when Jesus projected two incarnations of himself, Moses and Elias [Elijah], as well as his higher form as Jesus of Nazareth, the disciples witnessing this were able to see three projections of the same spirit on three separate occasions of soul evolvement. They were able to comprehend that

---

* *The Long-lost Second Book of Acts,* published in 1904, was discovered and translated by Dr. Kenneth Sylvan Guthrie. In 1990, Mark-Age issued a modern-English version, entitled *Seven Lives of Mary & Jesus: Second Book of Acts* (still in print).

the three were as one; but the three served different purposes at three distinct eras and evolutionary periods within the growth pattern of that particular spirit or I Am Self consciousness.

"It has become necessary in these end days of time for many to experience the various extensions or soul patterns of themselves at different parts of their unfolding. In order to do this they must come to the comprehension that all is under the control of the spirit or the I Am Self incarnate. In this period of comprehension, one can see or receive simultaneously several soul incarnations or patterns at a split second and can conceive of their purpose, of their interrelationship and of their various aspects."

Several points about the law of reincarnation are revealed in this communication. First, reincarnation is true. Second, information about past lives and past experiences from our soul records will be revealed to many of us, if they have not been already. Third, the purpose of soul revelations is to aid our spiritual evolvement. Fourth, this law allows us to incarnate repeatedly. In so doing we work to improve our own karmic situations as well as serve others.

Reincarnation is necessary for our growth and evolution, as explained in this communication by the apostle Paul on March 25, 1958: "Man grows and slips back, grows and slips back; seldom is it all in one direction. That is why we have the law of reincarnation, so man can repeatedly return to learn his lessons. When he learns a lesson he cannot unlearn it. It goes with him and he uses it, and thereby strengthens it by that use. He comes to learn certain other lessons which have been difficult for him. By practicing, suffering, living, he is taught and strengthened to grow in new directions, to overcome old, bad, useless habits."

One widely-held misconception about the interworking of three divine laws—growth and evolution, cause and effect, and reincarnation—is an idea called transmigration. This belief takes many forms throughout the world. But, in general, it is the view that living beings evolve into higher or lower orders of life in future incarnations depending on whether their actions are good or bad in their present life.

According to this conception, if a person lived an evil life he could in the next life be reborn as an animal or even as a plant or a rock. Conversely, a life form of a lower kingdom, say, a mineral, could evolve kingdom by kingdom into an angel if it accumulated enough good lifetimes.

The theory of transmigration is not true. Angels remain angels. People remain people. Animals, plants and minerals remain within their respective kingdoms. As children of God, the race of man works for the spiritual upliftment of the nature kingdoms. For millions of years we have utilized our Christ powers to unify with, and become one in consciousness with, individual or collective nature beings in order to learn how to interact lovingly with them and mutually evolve.

Communions with nature beings at this level of integration have been achieved and will continue. The memories of such experiences have their basis in truth. But in his mortal frame of mind, which emphasizes physical, material existence, man has misunderstood the memory of this spiritual activity and has construed it to be a physical reality. As a result, the false idea of transmigration was formulated.

An example of reincarnation for the purpose of serving others was given on May 6, 1960, by Zolanda, an Atlantean incarnation of Mary the Mother: "We are the White Brotherhood, that force dedicated to the salvation of the race on Earth. Many leave the Earth and evolve to higher spheres, but some are dedicated to remain Earthbound . . . for the advancement of the race of these men or sons of God. Many are reincarnated on Earth to serve as fellow beings; others remain in the etheric; and some go on to other planets."

There is a word for one who remains Earthbound in order to be of divine service to others. It is avatar. The name comes from the Sanskrit word *avatara,* which literally means "descent." Ascended masters, who are not compelled by the need to balance negative personal karma, become avatars when they incarnate over and over again on Earth to serve the race of man.

Returning to the words of Krishna, "Whenever dharma [manifestation of divine order] declines and the purpose of life is forgotten, I manifest myself on earth. I am born in every age to protect the good, to destroy evil, and to reestablish dharma."

One of the most important fulfillments of the law of reincarnation, besides being born, growing and evolving, is knowing why we are born. What is the purpose of our incarnation?

In a communication on May 3, 1961, Sananda-Jesus the Christ, spiritual leader of all who incarnate on and serve planet Earth, raises the same question: "I ask you, and suggest most earnestly and pleadingly: meditate upon this purpose; meditate upon the reason why you are here, why you have come into this life expression at this all-crucial moment for this particular planet.

"It is true that almost all of you have incarnated on this planet many, many times in the past for other reasons. Of course, you have incarnated in other planes and dimensions and on other planets as well, but we are not concerned with this. These are interesting proofs, these are interesting theories, but they do not serve your present-day needs unless they reveal to you the purpose of why you are here. Dwell on this, for I tell you we are going into the most important segment of time this planet has known in the last 206,000 years."

Let us ask this question of our I Am Selves and expect to receive an answer. We personally must fulfill this law like every other cosmic law. Just being born, remaining alive and making a living are not enough. We must accomplish the purpose for which we do all these things.

Let us always remember to affirm a most vital element of this eternal law: to be love incarnate. Wherever and for whatever reason we may incarnate in the universe, only when we are divine love incarnate can we be who we truly are: the I Am Self, the Christ, the only begotten Son of our Father-Mother God.

GROWTH & EVOLUTION

In the preceding chapter, we contemplated that reincarnation is an eternal principle because our growth and evolvement is oscillatory. We grow, slip back, progress and regress. Seldom does growth occur continually in one direction and without flaws. We reincarnate and, ideally, pick up where we left off.

In this chapter, let us examine growth and evolution in more detail because it, too, is a universal law. Everyone physically has experienced this law. So vast is its expression that we can only cover a few essential points.

Growth refers to an increase in size, weight, powers and complexity. It also means a gradual development toward maturity. In biology, individual growth is referred to as ontogeny, a process by which organisms develop and change form from a fertilized egg into an adult.

One misconception concerning positive, constructive growth processes is that they do not include errors or destruction. In many cases they do. Accepting this truth can take a lot of pressure off ourselves and those whom we must evaluate, such as our children or employees under us at work. Mistakes are an inherent part of this divine law; it is foolish to think that we have to develop perfectly in order to grow spiritually.

Cellular metabolism is a good example of this bipolar aspect of growth. Life-sustaining processes of cellular components and chemicals at the cell level are characterized by degradation as well as synthesis. Ecologists and people of primitive religions know this well: death, decay and transmutation are integral parts of the regenerative cycle of life.

In a nonphysical growth process known as the behavior of learning, trial and error is perfectly normal and natural. Any human behaviorist will agree that making errors is a legitimate part of the learning process.

All too often in Christianity and other religions, failure is equated with error and destruction, and therefore is considered a sin requiring punishment. A good indication of this is the use of the name Satan to refer to everything that is anti-God, anti-Christ or evil incarnate. *Satan* is derived from the Aramaic word *sata,* meaning "to slide," "to miss the mark," or "to go astray." Each of us has done that.

Certainly, many errors can be described as evil and even heinous. But the positive effect of errors in constructive growth processes often has not been acknowledged. Such misunderstandings have had a tremendously atrophic effect on man's mental, emotional, soul and spiritual development.

The attitude of the Hindu in this matter is vastly different from that of the Christian. Hinduism deifies death and destruction. Shiva, the Destroyer, is no less than the third person, or quality, of the Hindu trinity! The name Shiva *(siva)* means "auspicious," that which affords signs of a successful result. Shiva destroys the ego; but he also is the one who conquers death. What makes this very important for Christianity is that it recalls to mind the only figure in Christianity who conquered death: Jesus, of the Christian trinity.

Sananda-Jesus, in a communication on August 18, 1970, explains this aspect of the law: "In God's laws and methods there are life force, energy, growth; and a period of deterioration and dissolution when it becomes unto itself nothing but substance matter; and then re-forms and reenergizes into another or higher aspect of itself. For energy can never be lost; it is ever continuing. This is rightful progress. . . .

"But destruction, of itself, is not evil. For . . . the process of growth and evolution is a period of dissolution or consumption and re-formation. Therefore, the development stage of destruction, in a constructive process of growth, is not in itself evil or error. But man, seeing this process, partly understanding this process, has leaned toward this process and has named it evil."

True evil, then, is when the destructive or negative polarity of growth—which is to say, dissolution or disintegration—outweighs its positive pole, which is the constructive, integrating aspect. To have harmony in our lives, equilibrium between the two poles of this law must be maintained.

Too many positives in growth can be just as detrimental as too many negatives. On May 27, 1967, Archangel Michael explained this idea in more detail: "As the light within you grows and you can bear more and more light, you not only come closer to the Godhead but you open more and more to various potentials, talents and expressions. That is why you are not enlightened all at once. . . . For the light would so blind your particular potential or energy capacity that you would be unable to bear it and to utilize it constructively.

"Here then is the key to this particular unfoldment and revelation, that which is your own capacity for constructive growth. You must be able to use it constructively, which is good, which is for promoting the motion of life and light and truth and love, where you are in a manner that will serve not only your own growth and opportunities but serve the whole; as you are but a part of the whole, and the whole is concerned with each one of its parts. This is truth and eternal law.

"This is yours to master and to be mastered by. For each master accepts this understanding, uses this understanding and desires this procedure; for it is his own protection within the great universe of many laws, of many orders, of many means of structure. The law of God, the structure of God, is the same wherever you go. This is unchangeable and immutable. Thereby to master it in one place is to have the potential to master it elsewhere, though its form and its expression may deviate from what you are accustomed to and what you desire to entrance."

On the physical level, cancer is an obvious example of too much growth being destructive and potentially lethal. Since cancer cells do not respond to the body's normal regulatory factors, they grow and divide unchecked and invade healthy tissues.

Let us now turn to another aspect of this cosmic law: evolution, defined scientifically as the growth of groups of similar individuals through generations and over extended periods of time. In biological terms, this is called phylogeny—the evolutionary history of an organism as a species. The scientific theory or law of evolution governs the physical development of plant and animal life forms through time. It was adequately described for the first time by an English natural scientist, Charles Darwin, in his landmark work *The Origin of Species,* published in 1859.

Evolution, a process of adaptation of successive generations of organisms to changes in their environments, is without question true here on Earth. Because it is one aspect of a cosmic law, we would expect to find it operating even if we were living on another planet. According to Zorrah, a Neptunian king who communicated on January 3, 1963, we would be right: "You will find a lot of our organs to be similar to yours; but not everything, because our atmosphere on Neptune is entirely different than the atmosphere on Earth planet and we have adjusted naturally to our climates and so forth."

Currently, two main stumbling blocks to man's spiritual development surround the theory of evolution. One, that man—mind, body and soul—originated from out of the "primordial soup" of earth elements and is solely the product and highest expression of life that evolved on Earth, kingdom by kingdom, for billions of years. Two, that there is no inherent plan or purpose to evolution; that it is basically a directionless procedure with no end goal.

In 1871, Darwin published *The Descent of Man,* which extended his ideas on the random process of natural selection to human origin and evolution. Man descended or ascended, however one wishes to describe it, "from the apes," after millions of years of slow, gradual development from the dust of the Earth.

But given the physical changes of plant, animal and human life forms, what remain unresolved are those creations of man that cannot be explained by natural selection: art, music, mathematics, philosophy and religion. For many, these qualities of human culture indicate our transcendence of other forms of life. Consequently, in biology textbooks, cultural evolution is separated from "chemical" evolution.

"There is purpose, then, in what is, and in what happens in Nature." According to some scientific and theological analysts, this conclusion of Aristotle's, that living beings and their development have a divinely guided purpose, is one of the buckles of a straitjacket that Aristotle strapped on the mind of man and which endured for two thousand years.

The current scientific position on the purpose of evolution is given by Ernst Mayr, one of the finest biologists in the United States, in his book *The Growth of Biological Thought: Diversity, Evolution, and Inheritance:* "There is and never was any program [purpose] on the basis of which either cosmic or biological evolution has occurred. If there is a seeming aspect of progression in biological evolution, . . . this can be explained entirely as the result of selection forces generated by competition among individuals and species and by the colonization of new adaptive zones."

In a communication on October 24, 1971, Archangel Gabriel answers the questions raised by these two controversies—man's earthly origin and whether evolutionary development of life has purpose:

"Let us regress here and see what has happened to the race of man since the beginning of time or creation, when he was purely of the light and true essence of God in action. His descent into matter was but an experiment or a period of inquiry. Where he was required to know or to have knowledge, tasting both of the negative and the positive polarities of energy matter, he predominantly became enthralled with that which was of his own creation or ideas, not because he felt that evil or error was better than good or positive action but because he saw that there was an alternate route to all projected positive elements in his creative knowledge of life and life form. . . .

"This . . . is an example of what did take place in the beginning or genesis of your time on Earth, since you have it recorded in many scriptural references, regardless of race or religion you may be inclined to follow at this time.

"Man in his true spiritual evolution . . . was attracted unto the planet as you now know it, a third dimensional, physical, elementary origin of life substances and concepts. It was meant to be a house unto which certain animal and vegetable kingdoms were to develop and to experience higher life form. But because mankind—as you know, a son of God or the Light—came into responsible governing sharings, he substituted the plan and the principle by incorporating his own energy frequency in those animal forms. . . .

"But when he began to desire a control over all these lower beasts and to use the energy sources on the planet for his own manipulations and clarifications, he took an animal form that was more conducive to expansion and experimentation and rested his spiritual light force within it; which is a possibility and a prerogative of the higher energy forces, such as the light body or the spiritual, resurrected form. . . .

"By introducing himself into those animal forms, not one or two at a time but whole groups of them, he became involved in the evolutionary pattern of those forms."

All life today is participating in a divine plan whose goal is the enactment of the cosmic law we have been discussing: the spiritual growth and evolution of all planetary life forms in physical embodiment. Mankind has a special contribution to make to this tremendous coevolutionary process by adapting and growing into his next higher evolutionary form: the light body, through which our I Am or Christ consciousness functions fully.

Let there be love for our individual growth and humankind's collective evolution. Let us be still for a moment so that we perceive a truly great sight each and every day: the will of God as the divine law of growth and evolution unfolding on Earth through every living being.

ATTRACTION & REPULSION

What is the one cosmic law that can explain all the following diverse phenomena? A plant seed's ability always to send its first root growing down and its shoots growing up. How birds, porpoises and other animals orient themselves when they migrate. Why liquids are liquids and solids remain solid. Why the elements of our body behave the way they do; some stick together, some move around, and some are exchanged with our environment so that we can live and breathe.

All of these and other behaviors where force or energy is involved have at least one thing in common: the activity of the divine law of attraction and repulsion.

Gravity is an attractive force possessed by every material body, whether it be a planet or a mote of dust. The Earth's gravity causes starch crystals to be pulled to the bottom of root cells of sprouting plant seeds. This causes a growth hormone to be distributed within the root of a newly germinated seed so that it grows towards the center of the Earth. Known as geotropism, this directional growth is universal among terrestrial plants.

Animal migration is influenced by another force of nature that all forms of matter possess: magnetism. Scientists believe that tiny iron oxide crystals in near-brain tissues of birds align themselves north and south with the Earth's magnetic field, causing the appropriate neurons to fire so that the birds can navigate to their intended destination.

Electrical forces, both attractive and repulsive, are responsible for the different states of matter (gas, liquid, solid). Depending on the temperature and pressure of the environment, when mutual attraction between atomic elements (Van der Waals forces; ionic, covalent and hydrogen bonds, etc.) is weak, gases form. When it is strong, atoms and molecules form into solids. When the polar forces of attraction and repulsion are in the mid-range, liquids exist.

Attractive and repulsive electrical forces also are responsible for all of the metabolic processes in our bodies. Without this law, our anatomy and physiology would not be the same. Sight, hearing, touch, speech, and all pushing or pulling actions involve electrical or electromagnetic forces under the direct rule of the divine law of attraction and repulsion.

Any power whose action causes a drawing-toward comes under the definition of attraction. Attraction is the inherent tendency in all things to approach each other, to unite and to resist separation. Think of all the contexts in which you have heard these synonyms for attraction: inviting, alluring, engaging, attachment, dependence, affinity, desirable, tempting, bonding, captivating, cohesion, seduction, magnetic and enthralling.

At the other pole of this law, repulsion is the act of repelling, or the state of being repelled, of being pushed away from. It could be a strong dislike, distaste, aversion or repugnance to something. But not all synonyms of repulsion imply a revulsive or offensive quality. Think of these synonyms in the light of preventing harm from occurring, say, to our children: refusing, discouraging, declining, rejecting and detaching.

One of the significant aspects about this cosmic law is found in the definition of repulsion. It states that repulsion is the *mutual action* by which things tend to repel each other. This is also true about attraction. It takes two to repel and two to attract.

The whole truth, however, is that attraction and repulsion work together in mutual action. Although its name implies polarity, it is one single law. When one side of this law is put into effect, simultaneously the other side is also. For example, a person moving one step to the north not only draws one step toward the North Pole, he regresses one step away from the South Pole. The principle of attraction and repulsion clearly exhibits that a single action, that is, a single cause, *always* has more than one effect. Additionally, at least two of the effects will be diametrically opposed to one another.

In a channeling on March 14, 1962, John Mark explains attractive and repulsive forces: "Do you not see . . . that as you are raised to higher consciousness, as you feel greater love, understanding and feel a sense of rapport with the various levels of Christ kingdoms, these levels and forms then are magnetically attracted to you for further love and further cohesion? . . .

"So it is with those of a lower . . . understanding. Those forms, those creations which cannot be compatible to a Christ understanding and a Christ love that is developing within you, then are repelled by the vibrational frequency which you emit. It is like a perfume that comes from within you. Therefore, you also must take the responsibility of this rejection. You must take within you the responsibility that your state and level of consciousness has pushed away certain forces and elements which would otherwise be part of your existence, your understanding and your thoughts.

"All is One. Nothing in God's creation is separated. But you cannot be part of all, and you are not All. But you will, as you rise into a higher state of consciousness, be part of that equal level of consciousness in all other things, and be . . . rejected . . . from those which are of an incompatible set of vibrational frequencies. This applies not only to your physical visible world, as you know it in the third dimensional world, but it also applies to your invisible fourth dimensional world. It always has."

Spirit's power in heaven and on Earth always has this mutual action. This universal principle gives divine energy magnitude and direction. In man's case, when we love, we attract more love. The more loving we think, feel and act, the more love accumulates within us. As a result, our attractive power of love grows stronger. In essence, we become love.

This also means that by the law of attraction and repulsion our life is being repelled from hate, jealousy, retaliation and other error patterns. The desire to commit error is lessened by the same measure that we desire to love. There is no reason to struggle with error patterns within ourselves when, by working on our ability to love, automatically and permanently we repel evil. This is one explanation for Jesus' admonishment not to resist evil. He understood God's law of attraction and repulsion.

Man's misunderstanding or misuse of this law has produced serious consequences, as Archangel Chamuel explained on October 26, 1971: "It has been millions of years since the fall or the descent into matter by man, attracted by the selfishness, the self-love . . . of his desire to express for himself, to try evolution for himself, to flex his spiritual powers in his own way and for his own purposes and for his own selfish reasons.

"He saw, he knew, he felt the powers of the spirit within him and decided to experience them for himself and for his own advantages. . . . Man, who was attracted to this area because of the opportunities to conquer, to express and to show power over other and lesser forms, became entrapped by the very form he helped create or helped inaugurate."

Desire is a form of attraction. Selfish desire is attraction directed toward oneself and away from others. It can accumulate and become so intense that it can prevent us from loving others and sharing our lives and knowledge with them. We become like a human black hole from which Spirit's light within us cannot escape to help those in need.

Indeed, through selfishness we have drawn ourselves into a dimension of life whose lower vibrational frequency we never were intended to inhabit physically. Mankind is a race of spiritual beings whose true home is in the etheric realms, functioning in the light body. Our eternal residence is not in physical embodiment associated with the animal kingdom of Earth, however attractive that kingdom and physical life in some respects might be.

It should come as no surprise, then, that in various incarnations the spiritual leader and Prince of Earth, Sananda, has encouraged man to detach himself from thinking only in terms of mortal, physical existence. Instead, man should draw his thoughts back toward his true spiritual nature, the I Am Self.

In his dialogue *Phaedo,* Plato records what Sananda in his incarnation as Socrates considered mankind's greatest evil:

" 'What is this worst of all evils, Socrates?' asked Cebes.

" 'That the soul of every man is compelled, through experiencing some extreme pleasure or pain, to imagine that whatever most strongly arouses such feelings is most vivid and real—although, of course, it is not; and these things are chiefly the things that can be seen.' "

Sananda-Socrates is saying that simply because the bulk of our experiences and sensations are physical, we should not assign so great a significance to them that we identify ourselves with physical existence more than with our higher spiritual nature. That would be the worst thing we could do. As Jesus, Sananda rephrased this idea in the form of a question: "For how would a man be benefited, if he should gain the whole world and lose his own soul? Or what shall a man give in exchange for his soul?"

In his incarnation as Gautama Buddha, Sananda was not about to let man "lose his soul." In that magnificent life, he explained over and over again, in variations on a single theme, four noble truths that would lead mankind into enlightenment and help him "cross over to the other shore" of spiritual existence.

These are the four truths in simplified form: One, life is transient; our physical, mortal life is ever-changing and impermanent. Two, the source of all our suffering is attachment to and craving for sensual, physical desires and existence; in short, selfish desire. Three, there is a state of being in which we are released from physical attachments; this state can be achieved in this life. Four, the way that brings us out of selfish desire and into truth is an eightfold path called the Middle Way.

In Sananda-Gautama's second noble truth, the word *tanha* is used to indicate selfish desire or craving. *Tanha* literally means "thirst." Jesus said when drinking water at a well: "Everyone who drinks of this water will thirst again; but whoever drinks of the water which I give him shall never thirst; but the same water which I give him shall become in him a well of water springing up to life everlasting." In both incarnations, as Jesus and as Gautama Buddha, Sananda taught that man's true Christ being, wherein he lives selflessly for

Spirit, is his only permanent satisfaction. We have millions of years of physical existence as proof of that.

One of the words for the third noble truth, the truth of hope, is *tanhakkhaya,* "extinction of thirst." On the cross, Jesus said, "I thirst." Most certainly he was physically thirsty. Yet, he did not drink what was offered to him, for he thirsted more for Spirit. In other words, he desired Spirit and his I Am Self more than physical existence, or even the quenching of physical thirst.

He knew the law of attraction and repulsion well. For had his attention, his thoughts and desires been more for the physical, he would have repelled and prevented his demonstration of spiritual resurrection from physical existence.

When Christ Jesus spoke the words, "My kingdom is not of this world," he was not talking merely of himself. He was talking about each and every one who takes up physical incarnation on Earth. Our kingdom is not of this world.

In the book of Genesis, man's placement in the world is described this way: "And the Lord God planted a garden eastward in Eden; and there he put the man whom he had formed." Bible authority Dr. George Lamsa, in his book *Old Testament Light,* reveals that the term *Eden* is derived from *Edan,* which means "a moment" or "a season." In other words, Eden denotes a temporary period of time, inferring that spiritual man's physical stay on Earth is transient.

The implication of our transitory sojourn here is apparent in Jesus' remark to a man who said, "O my teacher, I will follow you wherever you go." Jesus said to him, "The foxes have holes, and the birds of the air a resting place, but the Son of man has nowhere even to lay his head."

These words, spoken as he was trying to withdraw from a large crowd, were more than an expression of tiredness or of itineracy. Jesus, the son of man demonstrating Christ consciousness while in a physical form, speaks of man's inability to reside–that is, to rest his spiritual being–permanently, eternally in a physical form on Earth. The birds and other animals, yes; this is their home world. But no person, no son of man, will find a place here to "lay his head." It is impossible. Mankind's period of inquiry, his physical evolvement on Earth, in Eden, is temporary.

Jesus said, "I, when I am lifted up from the earth, will draw every man to me." He was referring to the divine principle of attraction and repulsion within every son of God that enables us to draw others up with us into higher life, light and love expression. This is a universal truth and an inevitable manifestation of divine law. Of that, Jesus had no doubt and neither should we.

Our kingdom is not of this world. We, when we are lifted up, will lift all others with us. May we all realize this truth now, today, in remembrance of the Christ beings that we are.

RIGHTEOUSNESS

A question that probably goes through our minds at least once a day is, "What should I do? What is the right choice for me to make?" Within the cosmos there is a divine law which confirms there is a right choice and a wrong choice. It is the law of righteousness.

Righteousness is "the quality or condition of being righteous or just." To be righteous is to act in a virtuous, morally right or justifiable manner, to be good and authentic. *Rectitude* is the best synonym for righteousness. It means "correctness of method or judgment; strict honesty; straightness; uprightness of character." This is how the law of righteousness manifests in our lives.

For some, this law is so important that it is a matter of life and death. Living in an amoral and politically chaotic Chinese society in the fourth century B.C., the great Confucian philosopher Mencius wrote: "I like life and I also like righteousness. If I cannot have both of them, I shall give up life and choose righteousness. I love life, but there is something I love more than life, and therefore I will not do anything improper to have it." Mencius clearly believed in the principle of righteousness, one salient feature of which is that positive ends can neither completely nor permanently justify means that employ unjust practices.

For others, however, a universal law of righteousness cannot possibly exist. The ancient philosophical school known as the Greek skeptics denied the possibility of a general standard of conduct that could apply to all peoples and cultures. They supported their position by pointing to the wide range of human, social, ethical and political behaviors in Mediterranean cultures.

In the West, this gave rise to the idea of relativism. Relativism contends that differing views are not to be judged right or wrong nor good or bad by an absolute set of standards, but must be viewed within their proper context. Simply put, relativism states that what is good for one might not be good for another.

No one can deny that. We all know that what may be right or safe for an adult is not necessarily so for a child. What is good for a woman is not always good for a man. What is good for plants is not always good for animals or people.

If divine, ethical and moral values are relative, how could Confucius, the molder of Chinese civilization, say, "A superior man in dealing with the world is not for anything or against anything. He follows righteousness as the standard"?

How could Sananda-Jesus communicate through me on June 7, 1967, "I am not with you nor am I against you. I only am with the law of righteousness, the Lord God which dwelleth in each man, each nation and the world"?

How? Because there are divine laws which regulate life force throughout Spirit's creation; and righteousness is one of them. Truly, they are absolute.

As for relativism, its foundation rests on the truth that eternal, spiritual principles can be applied in an infinite number of ways. Just three of twenty-three cosmic laws—free will, individuality, and growth and evolution—create tremendous variations in lifestyles and social fabrics. Think what latitude in living the infinite combinations of all twenty-three laws bring.

On August 18, 1970, the Prince of this planet, Sananda-Jesus, communicated the answer to the question of the origin of good and evil: "It is on this basic question of good and evil that all progress and regression have been fought, have been struggled with and have been won. . . . There lives not a single soul who has not quested the rightful answer to this in his soul evolution and in the battleground of life eternal. So, let us now grasp a few concepts and make them steadfast in our eternal determination to give righteous and loving proof of the fundamental laws within this universe from which we are created and out of which we have our sustenance and existence.

"Let us begin first with the scriptural reference of the creation of all that may exist. In the beginning was the Divine Creator. Before this there was always the Divine Creator, or Principle Itself. So there never was a time, never can be a time, when this is not the fundamental reasoning and thought power.

"Out of this thought power and mind which is God, all has been created and has been sustained and has been put into motion, for good and evil. But all things were created before the evil even was mentioned. That is the sum and total of the entire question. It has not been the God Principle or Life Substance which created evil; but man, who contemplated the creation, who thought in terms of error or evil. . . .

"Let us not deceive ourselves that such conditions are only a matter of mental projections. For man is the Son of God. Under this regulation his mind power is very capable of creating a substance and matter out of his mind powers. So, by creating ideas and having thoughts independent of the role, the mission, the plan or the scheme of proper evolutionary progress and growth, he has created certain levels of being, certain creatures of being and certain deeds of being that are considered evil or erroneous to his proper growth and progress."

There is right and there is wrong. On an individual basis, there always is a good decision, a better action, a best choice, because simultaneously there is a poor choice, a bad course of action, a worse option. Almost always we will have a range of options from which to choose. But let there be no mistake. When we find our-selves in the middle of a confrontation, challenge or crossroads, there always will be an ascending scale of options on the side of right: fair, good, better, best. There also will be a descending scale of errant possibilities, the extreme of which is the worst case: evil.

This is why it is so important to know cosmic laws. We can apply them universally to every circumstance, thus helping ourselves to make the right choice.

Described by the noted translator and scholar T. W. Rhys Davids as "a turning-point in the religious history of man," Gautama Bud-dha's first teaching after achieving enlightenment was a detailed account of how to live the law of righteousness, known as the "Dis-course on the Foundation of the Kingdom of Righteousness." In it, Sananda-Gautama Buddha describes a noble truth about life: that although there is suffering in the world, there also is an eightfold path each person can travel that can put an end to all suffering, pain, misery, emptiness, imperfection and sorrow.

The Middle Way is a single path, but it has these eight integrated disciplines: right understanding, right thought, right speech, right action, right livelihood, right effort, right mindfulness and right con-centration.

Right understanding means having the right views about reality, having the right comprehension of cosmic laws and how they oper-ate. Proper understanding counteracts beliefs that lead to suffering. Examples of such beliefs include superstitions and delusions of vari-ous kinds, such as the idea that life is totally random and without purpose or meaning, or the belief that life is completely predeter-mined, so that our fate is sealed by the hands of other people, other gods, or God.

We express right thought as thoughts of love, compassion, mercy and nonviolence toward all living beings. Right thinking frees us from greed, hatred, selfishness and ignorance.

Right speech means not to lie, mislead, slander, gossip, or talk in any other impolite way. Rather, speak only truth in friendly and gentle ways. Say only what is useful and meaningful at the right time and in the right ways. Otherwise, be silent.

Right action involves abstaining from killing, stealing, dishonesty, illicit sexual contacts, and so on. In right conduct, we strive to love all beings, to be moral and peaceful, to have proper marital relations, and to help those in need.

Right livelihood involves maintaining our health, and acquiring our food, clothing, shelter and our living without harming others. We need to be able to acquire these things without preventing others from doing the same. For example, avoid professions where weapons are produced.

According to Buddhist monk and scholar Walpola Rahula, in his book *What the Buddha Taught,* the moral conduct generated by right speech, right action and right livelihood is requisite for all higher spiritual attainments. In fact, no spiritual development is possible without establishing morality in our daily lives.

Another key to the ending of suffering is right effort. Right effort involves our use of the divine law of free will. In right effort, we prevent evil from arising within us and society. We abandon evil already present. We promote good and protect and increase the good that already is present. Right effort is right use of will. It is patience, strength, and courage in the face of error.

For our effort to be right, we must have right mindfulness or attentiveness. Right mindfulness means being fully aware of and responsive to the actions and reactions of our physical, emotional, soul and mental bodies. Attentiveness to the continual changes in life helps us not to attach ourselves to worldly things to the point of disillusionment and suffering. Right mindfulness includes mental alertness, vigilance and a sense of responsibility.

Finally, we must have right concentration, which often is related to meditation. Right concentration does include different stages of achievement of yoga meditation, but it also means being able to focus our full attention on what we are doing so that we can do it right. Properly focusing our thoughts so that we are single-minded prevents us from being distracted and having scattered thoughts. With right concentration, we will be better able to perform our tasks perfectly and to fulfill our role and mission in life.

Roughly twenty-eight hundred years ago at Mount Carmel in the kingdom of Israel, Sananda, in his incarnation as the prophet Elijah, asked a huge gathering of people and priests, referred to as "all Israel" in the Bible, to choose which principles were right and true. They could choose the laws of God given to the prophets of Israel and handed down from generation to generation; or, they could choose a new form of pagan worship that was gaining favor in the region, Baalism. The Bible records the response of the multitude: "The people answered him not a word." They just didn't know. Well, that's history. The burden now is on us. Do we know?

A psalmist of the Old Testament who knew the answer gave this account of what the true laws of the universe meant to him or her: "The statutes of the Lord are right, rejoicing the heart; the commandment of the Lord is pure, enlightening the eyes. The reverence of the Lord is clean, enduring for ever; the judgments of the Lord are true and righteous altogether. They are more to be coveted than gold."

EXAMPLE

A familiar saying goes, "Do as I say, not as I do." Five centuries before the Christian era, Confucius taught, "The superior man is ashamed that his words exceed his deeds." Throughout the *Analects* of Confucius, the "superior man" is a literary device used to portray the character of a human being who sets a good example. There is a universal law that upholds this belief: the divine law of example.

Stephen Sander, a Sikh Canadian businessman, is a good example. In December 1989, after providing for his family, he gave away his fortune of one hundred million dollars, placing it in a trust fund to help the sick and starving in Third World countries. Mr. Sander returned to schoolteaching. But because he knows spiritual precepts and put them into practice, he already is a world teacher, particularly for the fortunate, by exampling the divine laws of give-and-take, sacrifice, love, free will, and other principles of Spirit.

In his gospel, St. John expressed the exemplifying of divine laws in one's life in terms of making the Word become flesh; that is, making the thoughts of Divine Mind, the principles of our Father-Mother God, an actual, tangible reality, as Christ Jesus did.

The dictionary defines *example* as "something selected to show the character or quality of the rest; a sample; a specimen; a person or thing worthy of imitation"; or "an instance of something to be avoided." An example is an instance that illustrates a principle, method, general rule or truth.

But to fathom the omnipresence of this law, we must refer to the definition and explanation of example given by Sananda on May 21, 1972: "As you are an individual, you still are a representative of a type of consciousness, a certain type of equation of experiences. . . . You have relations in family, sociological, national, religious, racial structures, even if it is the only incarnation in which you have participated in that particular race, religion, nation, family or sociological group. . . . You represent automatically all that is involved in that group consciousness, whether they be in the Earth or whether they be in the astral.

"You have not begun to comprehend the tremendous scope of each person's potential, of each person's responsibility and of each person's real functioning as a channel of God or as a son of God. . . .

"To give a very simple example of this, let us say you are a black writer in the United States whose parents or grandparents had been slaves brought over from Africa. You then represent all the slaves who were brought over from Africa; you represent the family group in which you are involved; you represent all writers in that particular category as a profession; you represent the United States of America in the particular aspect of that difficult sociological pattern.

"Therefore, anything you say and do, anything you experience, anything you achieve and anything you deny reflects back upon your own individual personal ongoing and record as a soul evolving from mortal into immortal expression. You also represent each and every one of those structures or groups who likewise are attempting to raise themselves from lower depths into higher consciousness and expression upon the Earth planet and into all eternity. This is the function you normally fulfill.

"It is the function every flower fulfills in its own species. It is the function every animal fulfills for its species. It is the function every mineral fulfills for the species or the type it represents. It is likewise so for every one of the elements as they grow or evolve into new patterns and equations for the fulfillment of the Creative Principle that is involved, which is our Father-Mother God. We all are the sons of It, the creation of this one Life Force."

Let us follow Sananda's guidelines and make a list of each grouping of people that we represent and for whom exemplifying spiritual law is the normal function we are to fulfill for them and ourselves. Judging from the above communication, it can safely be said that if every human being fully knew the extent of his obligations as an exemplar under this law, struggles for power, dominance and control would soon come to an end. For each would realize how full his plate truly is, without grabbing for more that is rightfully another's.

Example as a divine law means that we are continuously responsible to others. The higher in spiritual stature we climb, the more people we set an example for. But no matter where one is on the scale of spiritual development, each child of God is a representative pattern that others in some way will follow.

This principle does not choose for us which pattern we should follow. The divine law of free will gives us the freedom to choose any role model or any pattern we want. Ultimately, the perfect expression of this law manifests when we choose and then actually do God's will.

Our obligation under this law is twofold: first, to embrace the perfect pattern from which we all are cut—God's image and likeness; and second, to take that internal, divine pattern and externalize it for all those whom we represent and to whom we are responsible. All life forms are to live this law and to be good examples. This is what

108

Confucius meant when he said, "Let the ruler *be* a ruler, the minister *be* a minister, the father *be* a father, and the son *be* a son."

As we provide an example for others, so others provide an example to us; which is the other important aspect of this law. Whose example are we following now? Is he or she a proper role model? Whom are we to follow?

If we were Japanese snow monkeys living on Koshima Island, we would be following the example of Imo. Biologists who long had studied this troop of macaques set out sweet potatoes on the beach to supplement the monkeys' diet. Before their eyes, they saw a two-year-old macaque named Imo invent the practice of washing the sand off the potatoes in the ocean before eating them. Within ten years the majority of the troop learned to do the same.

The scientists also had been scattering edible grain on the sand. For two years the monkeys had picked it up one grain at a time. Again, it was Imo who made the breakthrough discovery. Imo gathered handfuls of sand and grain and threw them into the water. The sand sank, leaving the floating grain to be easily scooped up from the surface of the sea. Thus the troop learned another, more efficient harvesting technique. Even by human standards, Imo's exemplary behavior–discovering not one, but two entirely new ways of foraging which will benefit the welfare of the group for generations to come– is nothing short of heroic.

Throughout history, humankind always has had a seemingly infinite array of heroes, heroines, spiritual guides and authority figures. In mythic literature and legend, the Babylonian Gilgamesh, the Greek Achilles, the Celtic Amicus and Amelius, the English King Arthur, the Indic Karna and the Japanese Hiruko are a tiny sampling of heroes who exhibit desirable qualities.

The tradition of the spiritual guide, as a living example of a divine model for life, is in every major religion and higher philosophy. Historical figures like Pythagoras and Socrates are found in ancient Greek culture. The Jewish tradition contains true prophets of God, such as Moses and Elijah. In Christianity, there is Jesus. Gautama Buddha and *bodhisattvas* belong to Buddhism, and the patriarchal system serves a similar function in Ch'an or Zen Buddhism. The lama plays the same role in Tibetan Buddhism. The need of a disciple to find the proper *shaykh* or spiritual master was and still is of utmost importance for Sufis as well as orthodox Muslims. The same is true of finding a guru in Hinduism. These few examples point out the importance man has placed on role models and, therefore, on the divine law of example.

Yet, there are pitfalls in choosing a spiritual guide. The obvious mistake is choosing a poor example. Another pitfall is apotheosis, in which people make a god out of a person because he or she is a good example of divine traits. Apotheosis is particularly harmful when those of a low, impure consciousness are given divine status.

But as Sananda indicated on May 20, 1972, these setbacks must not discourage us from following a true leader, such as he was as Jesus: "But as Moses, Socrates, Melchizedek and Elijah, I also had given a number of expressions and experiences that would and could hold the light steady for that level and period of time, for those series of evolvements, and to bring about an education of the masses in a series of developments and sociological advancements and expressions. . . .

"That you are to follow and to remonstrate, as well as to demonstrate, is our purpose in setting forth these doctrines and examples in order that you may follow them and have a pathway safe and true unto your own evolvement and demonstrations for all who are in the race consciousness evolving from third into fourth dimensional expression."

In addition to all of the excellent secular and religious examples past and present that we can use to help guide us, Sananda explained on May 21, 1972, that there also is an internal pattern we need to exemplify:

"There is a simple measuring rod for all to follow. You each have the Christ Self within, which guides, protects and leads your individualized soul expression. . . . You each are capable of seeking the guidance and the instruction from the Christ Self within, regardless of whether you are aware of the contact and regardless of whether you are sure of the spiritual union of the Christ Self with the mortal self. Therefore, it is your requirement and it is our desire that you seek this over and above all other yearnings and instructions. Regardless of who the teacher is upon the Earth, regardless of who the teacher may be, including myself, upon the etheric or the celestial planes, you must seek and unify with that Christ Self within you."

Does this really mean that we should seek guidance from our higher Self over and above our human guides whom we greatly admire and with whom we physically can communicate? Should we seek spiritual instruction first from our Christ Self over and above the greatest living examples in this solar system—Lord Maitreya, Archangel Michael and the rest of the spiritual Hierarchy? Should we seek contact first with our own I Am Self instead of with Sananda himself?

The answer is yes. This is the awesome and magnificent meaning of Jesus' simple command to his disciples: "Follow me." Follow me not only because of who I am as a leader, the Prince of Earth. Follow me not only because my life exemplified the way, the power and the principles of Spirit. Follow me because I am the example of the Christ Self within every one of us, who says: Follow me; follow my instruction, the divine guidance available to you always.

Why is this instruction emphasized so much by every true spiritual master? Sananda gave the answer as he continued his previous discourse: "For until you [seek and unify with that Christ Self within you] and until you have begun the anchoring of the light body with the physical, the mental and the emotional bodies of your mortal expression, the immortality of your spiritual Self shall not be realized. . . . Regardless of whom you seek, regardless of what path you follow, regardless of whom you rely on for your strength, there is no other more secure, more important than your own spiritual Self within.

"The immortality of your own individual expression has to be the Christ or higher Self within you unified with the mortal and the subconscious areas of your self-expression. It is not beyond our ability

111

to bring this unification process to your attention. But it is beyond our ability to solidify and to insure a final and lasting anchorage of the spiritual Self with the mortal self. That has to come from within the individual's consciousness each time, no matter how many times it has been performed, has been learned and has been accepted in the past.

"Each step of the way, each repetition of the unification of the spiritual with the mortal has to be done from within the individual's consciousness and by his own self-will to accept, to work with, to cleanse and to transmute the personality self or the mortal consciousness with the immortal or spiritual I Am Self presence."

This is the point of law where personal responsibility enters. Nobody else can anchor our light body and higher consciousness for us. No one can provide an example for all those we represent as powerfully and as completely as we can. What if we should fail? There always have been and always will be alternates who will stand in when vacancies occur. But when we are guided by Spirit through our Christ Self, we are the best, both for ourselves and for those whom we serve by example.

Let us, then, be love in example. For God so loved the world that He gave all His sons, every child of Spirit, one to another; so that whoever believes in his God Self should not perish, but have eternal life. Heavenly Spirit, thank You for all of us.

BALANCE & HARMONY

These are the words of Lord Michael, the angelic head of this solar system's government: "Our solar system is in the western part or the declining part of a higher order of being. There are many life forces in other parts of the universe of which our solar system is but one small segment. These forms and races have a need to evolve to another sphere of development. Our solar system, being on the western hemisphere or the negative half of balance of the two parts, must come up to its standards within a certain sphere of time and cycle of events.

"Naturally, the power of this universe is beyond anything we have informed you about until now, because you could not utilize any of the information or do much about it. But since the Earth is the laggard in the solar system, the solar system is a weak link in the chain within the western hemisphere of this universe of which it is part.

"So, first things first. Bring up the Earth; cleanse and balance the solar system history and events; then join in with the rest of this universe in brotherhood and usage of powers concomitant with that."

In this communication through me on July 9, 1969, Lord Michael expressed one cosmic aspect of balance and harmony: species of life throughout the various realms of God's creation express this law in unique ways. To those of us on Earth, balance can mean bodily equilibrium where all the physiological systems of our physical body are working properly. Thus, balance expresses health rather than disease or death. Balance also refers to our mental body and our emotional body by implying mental and emotional equilibrium.

Our soul or astral body carries the record of our experiences, our karmic credits and debits. This refers to yet another meaning of balance: the quantity of weight or a sum that is necessary to bring something back into balance or equipoise. Karma is the sum effect, present and past, of everything we personally cause, create or influence. When we reincarnate, we balance debits or errors in whatever form they may take. Furthermore, we receive credits that enhance our lives.

Too often, we have a negative view about the need to reincarnate. We believe that we are returning somewhere because we have done something wrong that needs correcting. But in many cases, our return is a positive opportunity to do something right. A balanced view of life and reincarnation was expressed by Jesus in a communication on December 12, 1961:

"Without the projection of divine love, peace and divine power, we cannot keep the Earth in its orbit with relationship to the planets of this solar system. That is why so many have volunteered to incarnate, where there was no need for self-discipline or self-evolvement into Christ awareness. Unless there is on the planet itself the balance of love and power being projected from the plane on which you are presently demonstrating, it could not go through the extremely cataclysmic changes which are necessary to sweep it clean and to begin afresh.

"Therefore, many who were responsible on other planes and planets of this solar system, of this galaxy and other universes hearkened to the need, because if one single planet or cell is out of order the entire universe and universes are thrown out of their own balance of order and harmony in the scheme of God's divine beingness."

More of us than we think are here on this planet for only good and positive reasons. Our coming together to serve one another with love to help maintain the Earth's balance in these Latter Days is a perfect expression of the cosmic law of balance and harmony.

Harmony denotes a fitting together, a joining of diverse combinations of things into an orderly, proportionate whole. Promoting agreement in feeling, action, ideas and interests, harmony fosters peace and friendship. Consonance of energy, sound, color, shapes and movement creates beauty and pleasure.

Sananda-Jesus reminds us of a great truth with respect to this law that we must never forget. We all know of the negative things that are happening in the world today, the catastrophes and cataclysms. But these dire events are allowed to take place because an equally proportionate amount of positive love and light is present in the world. So, whenever we hear of something that is wrong, let us remember this law and realize that somewhere Spirit already is expressing its positive counterbalance. This is accomplished through people of high ethics, morality and spirituality, who are the positive embodiment of the law of balance and harmony, and act as the counterpoise for Spirit within the race of man.

Largely as a function of our subconscious, our physical body almost automatically maintains the principle of balance and harmony. The term biologists and medical physiologists use for the expression of this law is *homeostasis*. Arthur C. Guyton, M.D., Professor and Chairman of the Department of Physiology and Biophysics at the University of Mississippi School of Medicine, has written one of the standard textbooks on medical physiology. In his opening chapter, he describes homeostasis and just how important it is for life:

"The term *homeostasis* is used by physiologists to mean 'maintenance of static, or constant, conditions in the internal environment.' Essentially all the organs and tissues of the body perform functions that help to maintain these constant conditions. For instance, the lungs provide oxygen as it is required by the cells, the kidneys maintain constant ion concentrations, and the gut provides nutrients."

Further on, he writes: "The body is actually an *aggregate of about 75 trillion cells*. . . . As long as normal conditions are maintained . . . the cells of the body will continue to live and function properly. Thus, each cell benefits from homeostasis, and in turn each cell contributes its share toward the maintenance of homeostasis. This reciprocal interplay provides continuous automaticity of the body until one or more functional systems lose their ability to contribute their share of function. When this happens, all the cells of the body suffer. Extreme dysfunction leads to death, while moderate dysfunction leads to sickness."

Medical researchers have discovered four ways our physical body maintains its balance and harmony. Using this as an analogy for conscious action, we can apply in our outer life the same means our subconscious employs every moment to maintain balance and harmony within our body.

1. Acquire and transport needed nutrients. Each cell takes only what it needs and does not hoard or rob nutrients needed by other cells. We as a race must do the same to balance this Earth. Essentially, this involves eliminating greed and being willing to make sacrifices and to love one another.

2. Remove metabolic end products. Cells constantly release undesirable compounds or waste. Likewise, we constantly should eliminate

115

erroneous beliefs and unwanted negative emotions, such as hatred and the like. Forgive every day.

3. Regulate body functions. The body's nervous and hormonal systems regulate by being sensitive to the needs of each cell, integrating that knowledge and causing other organs and systems to respond to each need. In the same way, we also must remain aware of both our personal needs and the needs of others. We must be able to cooperate with each other, responding adequately and in a timely manner to fulfill those needs on a continuous basis.

4. Reproduce. Life maintains itself by creating new life. We need to be involved daily in creative work that produces life outside of ourselves, that creates life-giving energy or life-fulfilling products for others, for society or for the natural world. Daily enjoy some form of recreation. All these means perpetuate balanced and harmonious life.

Sananda-Jesus delivered additional important keys to this law on February 26, 1962: "Nowhere in our communications have we ever issued ultimatums, but have given you full freedom of choice and free will to serve the Creator or your individual selves.

"Now we have the ultimatum in readiness before we can instigate another unfoldment to the plan . . . : at no time can you waver in consciousness for the negativity of balance while demonstrating Christ consciousness. This not only would endanger your soul evolvement and the entire structure or balance of the etheric bodies with the subconscious and conscious planes, but it would cause destruction to the planet upon which you are to manifest group Christ potentials and fulfillment. . . .

"Surely our instruction is positive, but negative influences must be honored before they can be eliminated by your own decreeing and fullness of understanding where their position is controlled by the law of balance and harmony. In all ways, the Christ anointed must have full control and consciousness of the conflict, which is another word for a balance between the two poles of power. At no time may the anointed ones give their credulity to overlap. In every case, power must be controlled without ever emphasizing action of light.

In other words, light must be projected only in proportion to the amount of negation prevalent in the existing situation as it manifests temporarily on the plane where it places its control. Now you have the higher law."

In optimal conditions, seventy-five trillion cells of our body each moment receive the exact amount of nutrients they need, no more and no less. So, too, in our elimination of personal and planetary errors: the optimum manifestation of this higher law requires that we use only the needed amount of love, light and life energy. For God does not waste.

Spirit gives us great freedom in how we choose to solve disharmonies and imbalances. But in one case, our free will must not deviate from Spirit's will. Never should we accept or condone negativity in any form: in thought, in feeling, in method or in action. We must wholeheartedly stay on the positive side of the balance.

As adamant as Sananda-Jesus is on this matter, he instructs us that in order that errors may be eliminated, negative influences must be honored. Honoring the negative enables us to distinguish and recognize what is wrong so that we can make adjustments to balance it.

The position of all the negative influences in us and in the world—their place, their status, their rank or order of importance—is controlled by this law of balance and harmony. At every moment, Spirit and Its agents act as a divine counterforce for us until we learn, in each and every case, how to use properly God's energy according to divine, cosmic standards.

When we have full control and awareness of conflict, we are able to create balance between the two poles of power. In every case, the two poles of power refer to the dual character of Spirit's Divine Being: God the Father and God the Mother. In principle, these two poles embody the divine law of polarity. God the Father represents the positive, masculine aspect; God the Mother represents the negative, feminine aspect. Together, they both exist in all energy and forms throughout the universe.

In God, man has a perfect example of how to live in balance and harmony. For Spirit is balance and harmony on all levels of Its expression. On October 17, 1962, Lord Maitreya channeled: "It is, in truth, that man is created of a balanced Creator or Spirit which projects Itself positively and negatively, or in a male or female vibration. . . . Never is Spirit imbalanced, nor can It ever be, because It projects out into Its creations the various weights and balances to keep It so poised in the center of purity, harmony and truth."

As children of God, we were created balanced by the love of God, which always creates a balanced reaction between Its positive and negative polar nature. How then do we create in balanced, harmonious and loving ways?

John Mark answers this question in a message on January 17, 1961: "If the exchange of life force on the spiritual, mental or physical levels is for the exchange of spiritual energies or for high Self expression or for the payment and the deposit of energies, we find it is for the enhancement of the individual expression in whatever realm it is expressing itself. For these are but means that Spirit has of depositing and withdrawing Its own complementary force fields.

"The so-called sexual exchange is a creative act on any realm; which is quite obvious on your physical realm, not so obvious on your mental realm and more illusive on your spiritual realm when viewing it with the consciousness of the Earthman's conception.

"On the mental realm it is the positive and negative thought-balancing to create a thought form that is perfect, neither too much of the negative nor too much of the positive. . . . This applies to an individual working on a creative project alone or to more than one individual working out a new pattern together. The balance, the harmony must be set up in the thought or mental imagination realm.

"On your spiritual realm it is that sense of divine love feeling and the divine love action, perfectly balanced, perfectly harmonious, that creates a higher form or a higher ideal, a new dimension into which man or any of God's creation can step. This of course is the purpose of the physical exchange: to bring forth higher form, greater evolution in the physical concept of the life on the planet.

"In the time to come, when we step into the Golden Era and man and woman on Earth can spend and receive all three levels simultaneously and with the same purpose, you will have the intunement of Christ-conscious awareness in alignment not only with each to himself but each to one another. Then will the planet know real peace, real harmony, perfect love for the Divine, perfect love for the Energy which is Spirit and Spirit which is Energy.

"Thereby the second commandment can be fulfilled, the commandment of *Love One Another,* for then you are loving Spirit in self and in each other manifestation of Spirit. This truly is Christ consciousness. Then is the true exchange, the true realization, the free flow in and out, spending and receiving, giving and taking, Spirit in action, love in action."

Spirit also creates in a balanced and harmonious way because the divine energy and thought radiations It uses are themselves balanced. Members of the Hierarchy use the term *balance* to describe each of Spirit's seven principal powers, attributes or activities, which they refer to as the Seven Flames or Rays of Life. From channeled communications in the Mark-Age booklet *Seven Rays of Life,* here are some ideas that we immediately can use to regain and maintain balance and harmony in our lives.

Working with issues of First Ray will and power, we must remember that there are two legitimate aspects to our will. The negative aspect is self-will, the will to sustain one's life and survive as an individual. The positive aspect represents the will of God, which includes concern for all life. The key is, we should never favor one over the other but should try to balance and harmonize the two so that they complement each other. This harmony correctly is expressed as following Spirit's will so as to benefit both self and others.

Mental balance, the harmonious functioning of various aspects and powers of the mind, is an expression of the Second Ray of Life. Our superconscious aspect of mind must be balanced with subconscious and conscious aspects. Wisdom can only be expressed through even-mindedness. Levelheaded tolerance of others enables all sides of a conflict to be honored and fully understood so that a solution can be found.

Third Ray balanced expression is the burning desire to love

divinely. The Director of the Third Ray for the race of man in this solar system, Lanto, personally requests that, in order to maintain balance, we concentrate on the color radiation of a particular ray when we are working with that ray's corresponding human activity.

When meditating on subjects pertaining to First Ray will and power, visualize the color blue. On concerns relating to Second Ray wisdom and understanding, visualize the color yellow; for Third Ray personal love and feeling, the color pink. The Fourth Ray, comprising crystallization and manifestation, is clear (colorless). Green is the color of Fifth Ray unity and integration. In Sixth Ray activities of cleansing and transmutation, project the color violet. Finally, white and gold are the most appropriate colors in situations involving Seventh Ray divine love, peace and rest.

The Fourth Ray is characterized by anything, especially thought, that is equally balanced in physical man. A balanced thought is a clearly understood thought. The most balanced and harmonious way we can manifest our spiritual inspirations and ideas on Earth is to accept our physical reality and our metaphysical or spiritual reality simultaneously. We should not reject the existence and the workings of either one in our lives.

Whenever we are involved with Fifth Ray activities, we are involved with integration: integration of superconscious, subconscious and conscious aspects of mind; of peoples and nations of the world; of other planes and life forms in the universe, and so forth. Just by accepting the oneness of Spirit in all these ways, we gain more balance, stability and harmony in our life.

St. Germain, the Hierarchy's Sixth Ray Director, says that the word *transmutation* means "balance." Yet, he cautions us to be very sure about what we pray to be balanced in us. Why? When we ask for balance, Spirit responds by informing us where the blockage lies within. This can be very upsetting. It might be something painful in our past or something we did not know about ourselves and that we may not like. Hence, caution is recommended when we request transmutation.

Through Seventh Ray expression of life, Spirit in us supplies the most significant key in gaining balance, harmony and full control of any conflict. The key is divine love. On February 13, 1963, Sananda, Director of the Seventh Ray, explained:

"We are in the Seventh Ray activity of life or light known as peace, tranquillity, balance or harmony. . . . Why is it that love and peace are one? Because as love is brought forth into its fullest balance—coordinated with its six other levels of consciousness, steps or forces—then peace is achieved within the individual life stream. Peace, balance or harmony is achieved with the six other forces. . . . It cannot happen overnight. Therefore, I ask that you begin to see this seventh step, this love vibration within you, coming forth stronger and stronger. For it is through the seventh step, the final step of love, that all others are controlled in actuality. . . .

"You who are part of the Earth, demonstrating and finding fully your own balance and harmony as individual cells or souls and thereby bringing the whole Earth into a joyous love and peace on Earth, then will balance out the entire solar system."

COMPENSATION

All of the divine laws of Spirit are already a part of the structure of our being, for God is within each of us. We need only allow our mind and heart to materialize them so that we can fulfill our true destiny: to act in the image and likeness of God. Such is the case with the divine principle of compensation. Since our origin, we have been endowed with a natural tendency to compensate fairly in return for something received, just as Spirit does throughout Its creation.

To man's credit, it is one of the few cosmic laws that have been given wide recognition within our legal systems. Understood to mean something that is given or received as an equivalent for services, debt, want, loss or suffering, compensation is evident in many of our laws, including workers' compensation, accident liability, copyright infringement and defamation of character, just to name a few.

Psychologists point out that when people attempt to disguise undesired traits by exaggerating desired or socially approved traits, they are exhibiting compensatory behavior. So, we "grin and bear it," "put our best foot forward," or "put on a happy face" in order to mask our true mental and emotional states.

Man also has uncovered the principle of compensation in the world of nature. For example, in the mineral kingdom there is what geologists term the law of isostatic adjustment. This occurs where large areas of the Earth's crust had been depressed topographically by heavy accumulations of ice during the Ice Ages. As the ice melted and its weight was transferred to the ocean basins, the land areas compensated by slowly buoying back up. The process continues to this day.

Plant physiologists have been able to describe types of compensation in the plant kingdom. Consider, for instance, plants growing in soils low in nutrients. In order to supply essential elements to fast-growing shoots and leaves, plants compensate for elements unavailable in the soil by translocating them from mature older leaves.

Biologists recognize the principle of compensation when a physiological defect in the structure or function of a body part is counterbalanced by greater activity or development of another or several other parts.

Compensated heart failure is a good example of how this principle works within the same organ. To put it simply, when an acute, moderate heart attack occurs, the heart may fail to pump blood adequately. Automatically, the sympathetic part of the autonomic nervous system strengthens the damaged musculature and strongly stimulates the remaining normal muscle. This causes the heart to become a stronger pump, up to double from the damaged state.

Mortal man's conception of the universal principle of compensation emphasizes the divine law of equality. Our laws stress equivalent payment for services, loss or sacrifices.

Jesus' instructions to his disciples acknowledged the legitimacy of equality as one component of compensation. When he sent out the twelve apostles to teach and to heal, he told them, "Do not accumulate gold or silver or brass in your purses; . . . for a laborer is at least worthy of his food." But Jesus knew that compensation understood from the perspective of only one cosmic law—equality—would manifest only a portion of this law, in his own words, only the "least" amount. Combining compensation with all of the other laws of God, with the totality of Spirit's will, can produce much more, *if* man only has faith in all the divine laws.

Lord Michael channeled to El Morya-Mark and me, the Mark-Age cofounders, on April 27, 1969: "You have announced independently that you have only the pledge and purpose for enacting God's will upon the Earth in the present life span. This will be exacted from you by Spirit and returned unto you blessed and multiplied; that your life span will be full of joy, full of activity, full of reward, according to the spiritual concept of remuneration [compensation] and not according to man's understanding of remuneration or blessings."

Clearly, then, when we surrender to the will of God, all the principles of Spirit create a multiplication effect when compensation is divine.

For us, this multiplication factor expresses itself in many different ways. Consider cases of forgiveness, for example, where we must compensate for the wrongs and the failings of others. The apostle Peter asked Jesus, "My Lord, if my brother is at fault with me, how many times should I forgive him? Up to seven times?"

Jesus replied, "I do not say to you up to seven times, but up to seventy times seventy-seven." Interpreted literally, Jesus is saying to Peter: Do not just forgive somebody seven times, but 5,390 times! In other words, forgiveness always is required of us; it is an eternal activity, a principle of Spirit. To be true to ourselves and to God, we must learn to forgive the shortcomings of others, as well as our own mistakes.

When we make sacrifices for the good of the whole, divine compensation manifests as a multiplied reward for services rendered. This was the case of a Mark-Age leader in 1973. Here is part of Sananda's January 24 soul intunement to him, delivered through me:

"Your own karmic evolvement will accelerate speedily because you have accepted more responsibility than was intended at this particular time for your own growth and expansion. . . . For you have accelerated in a number of directions, but have been decelerated from fulfilling certain soul-evolving patterns and talents. Because of this sacrifice, your accelerated pace of understanding and functioning will be your compensation, because this is how Spirit does reward those who sacrifice personal self for the overall spiritual need of others and the higher goals of mankind at large."

From this instruction we all can be assured that when we enact the divine law of sacrifice, our compensation by Spirit will be multiplied far beyond what we can imagine. In retrospect, what we have given up will seem insignificant in comparison.

What are some of the key elements required of us so that we may fulfill this law? In a channeling on April 27, 1969, from my high Self, it was explained we must have faith that all of our work and demonstrations—through the thousands of years of evolvement and repeated incarnations in which we have restated truth principles—have had a worthwhile and fruitful effect on mankind:

"It must be according to that set standard, because without it we would not be fulfilling the divine law of compensation: that which you have put forth in effort sincerely, purely and without guile or desire for recompense must be doubled in the return of spiritual grace and function."

Enacting this law divinely requires sincerity: being truthful, faithful, straightforward, honest and genuinely the same within as without. It requires purity: being clear, simple rather than a mixed-up jumble of thoughts and emotions, and free from anything that impairs or taints us.

We have to be without guile. This means we cannot be cunning, artificial, duplicitous or deceitful. To act in perfect accord with this

124

law, we must be without any desire for recompense; even though we know full well that Spirit will double our good fortune when we live this law to the letter. Divine compensation requires that we be purely selfless.

Here is the signal key to the prosperity consciousness which is so much in vogue with New Thought and New Age groups today. We cannot be concerned primarily about our own self-serving prosperity, but rather the prosperity of others. As with all other divine laws, selfishness adulterates this law.

Jesus addressed this aspect of the law when he described the kingdom of heaven as being like a landowner who hired laborers to work in his vineyard. From early morning until late in the day he hired them. When it came time for payment, the ones who had worked all day expected to be paid more, but were not. After hearing their complaints, the landowner said: "I am not being unfair to you. Didn't you agree to work for a denarius?* Take your pay and go. I want to give the man who was hired last the same as I gave you. Don't I have the right to do what I want with my own money? Or are you envious because I am generous?"

In this parable, Jesus taught exactly what Lord Michael stated earlier: Spirit's concept of compensation is not the same as man's limited concept of equivalence in remuneration. God's compensation is benevolent; always infinitely more generous than we can expect.

When we have spiritual grace—when we add to our disposition the ability to grant things freely to others, with goodwill, mercy, decency and propriety—Spirit will multiply our supply, for we have proved ourselves to be a worthy supervisor and a pure vessel through which our Father-Mother can work.

In the Bible, this multiplication of Spirit is not the spirit of the law, but the letter of the law. It was the letter of the law in the time of Moses, in the time of Elijah, as well as in the time of Jesus. Without a doubt, it is the letter of the law for us today. The response of the autonomic nervous system during compensated heart failure,

---

* *Denarius:* a Roman silver coin that was the ordinary pay for a day's labor.

cited earlier, reveals how literally—unto the doubling of power and function of a damaged physical organ—Spirit's law manifests. If this is true of our physical form, how much more so must it be true of the thoughts and feelings of our mental and emotional aspects. Truly, those who express selfless acts of love and kindness will receive compensation as *only* Spirit can give.

Words can hardly express the vast difference between compensation as mortal man has conceived it in his laws, and compensation as Spirit has decreed it in cosmic law.

Maybe this anecdote from the New Testament will elucidate. A vivid exchange concerning the divine law of compensation took place between Peter, who symbolically portrays faith in God's laws and in the Christ, and Jesus, who exemplifies I Am Self consciousness. Distressed after years of sacrifice, with the prospect of facing an untold number of hardships ahead, Peter exclaimed: "We have left everything and followed you; what will we have?"

Jesus replied: "Truly I say to you that in the new world when the Son of man shall sit on the throne of his glory, . . . every man who leaves houses or brothers or sisters or father or mother or wife or children or fields, for my name's sake, shall receive a hundredfold, and shall inherit everlasting life."

LIFE

"His commandment is life everlasting; these things therefore which I speak, just as my Father told me, so I speak."

These words of Jesus lead us into one of the fundamental laws of the cosmos: the divine law of life. Except perhaps in cases of serious illness, most of our lives we do not give much thought to the fact that we are alive. We exist, we think, we move, we wake up every morning as if such acts were automatic.

Yet, if we were asked, "What is life?" we probably would react as

St. Augustine did when he was asked, "What is love?" He replied that he knew what love was until he was asked to define it.

The dictionary will give us a definition: *life* is "that property of plants and animals which makes it possible for them to take in food, get energy from it, grow, adapt themselves to their surroundings, and reproduce their kind."

When we pursue the subject of life further, we discover something astonishing. After thousands of years of life and in spite of an enormous deluge of scientific information about life, man has come to no generally accepted definition of life. Anatomists, taxonomists, physiologists, ecologists, geneticists, embryologists, evolutionary biologists, and other scientific and nonscientific groups all have their specific perspective on life.

Since prehistoric times, the most important sign of life has been breath. In the Bible, for example, God is described as having breathed into Adam's nostrils the breath of life; only then did Adam become a living being. Yet, today the pulse beat of our heart and our brain wave activity measured by sophisticated instruments are the accepted and dependable methods to determine the presence of life.

Our modern scientific equipment, on which we depend, is only sensitive to certain kinds of life. In a communication on November 7, 1962, my I Am Self stated: "Scientists today are saying that in many ways they cannot see how life could exist on another planet because of various physical conditions. They are absolutely correct, it could not exist. Our physical bodies could not exist on other planets in this solar system as they are evolved at this particular time. But those planets have life forms in another dimension and in another frequency that are not possibly seen by the physical instrumentation the scientists today are using. . . .

"Your own etheric form is entirely different than your physical form, both in feeling nature and in visual quality. It has transparency. . . . It has the ability to materialize and to dematerialize, to expand and to shrink. It has the ability to take on various colors."

Obviously, this information about life won't be written into biology textbooks until sometime in the twenty-first century, after the Second Coming. But at present in man's quest to understand life, monumental efforts are being exerted.

One such example is the Human Genome Project, begun in 1990 and completed in 2003. Its goal was to map all three billion units of genetic information present in human chromosomes. One result is that medical science now has yet another powerful tool for preventing disease. Extensive follow-up research continues. Project staffers state that "deriving meaningful knowledge from DNA sequence will define biological research through the coming decades."

While the massive international effort was under way, project worker Leroy Hood said: "It's, in a sense, the Holy Grail of genetics. What we will have done, when we have the human genome initiative completed, is we will have written out the book of life, and that will be basically the hardware of how you construct a human being."

Certainly this is a remarkable achievement in the life sciences, made possible only with the help of new technology. But equally remarkable is the achievement of a fading aboriginal culture in Australia, the Kakudju, who undoubtedly do not know about the Human Genome Project. Insofar as anthropologists can determine, their legacy to the world is to have lived in the same place for forty thousand years without diminishing any of their local environment's abundant and diverse plant and animal life.

This is a stunning demonstration of living the law of life—one that technologically advanced, "civilized" societies have never matched. But the Kakudju are not mere *Homo sapiens*. Neither are we, for that matter. Like us, they are *homo religiosus*.

J. Bruce Long explains this distinction in his summation on "Life" in *The Encyclopedia of Religion:* "In the view of *Homo sapiens,* mere physical survival has never stood as an adequate legitimation of human life. . . . For *homo religiosus,* a meaningful life is predicated upon the confidence that the world and all the creatures who inhabit it are the handiwork of divine creative forces or beings. . . . Thus, humans everywhere look to a transhuman order of being for the revelation of the basic structure of the universe and of the moral and spiritual laws that govern its various operations."

Now is the time for all on Earth to conduct their lives as a true affirmation of the divine law of life; not only in its physical aspects with which we all are familiar, but in the transhuman order of this phenomenal law as well.

According to Archangel Jophiel on October 25, 1971, the source of life is: "Man is a son of God, . . . divinely projected from the source of life, which is the law of God." In his prayer at Passover (the Last Supper), Jesus spoke similarly of life: "Father, the time has come. Glorify Your Son, that Your Son may glorify You. . . . Now this is eternal life: that they may know You, the only true God."

Earlier in his travels, Jesus was asked by a wealthy young man, "O good Teacher, what is the best thing that I should do to have life eternal?" Jesus answered, "If you want to enter into life, obey the commandments." Then he listed the commandments Moses had received on Mount Sinai. (Christ Jesus did not reveal that he had been Moses in a previous incarnation.)

The point is that we can be alive and still not be living fully the law of life, which is the only true living. Only when we follow cosmic laws, which are the expression of God's will, will we be thinking, feeling and acting according to timeless cosmic standards. When we live according to them, our life takes on the same eternal quality. It is at that moment, no matter where we exist in the cosmos, that we "enter into life" everlasting.

We owe our existence to God and to the elohim, those beings at the head of each ray of life. Jesus informed us about our living relationship with the elohim on March 19, 1969: "Beyond the angelic realm are the Seven Flames of Life or elohim, the lights or the light of God seven times manifested, each giving expression to one or more aspects of the God Force. . . .

"We begin, in all evolution, with the elohim; who speak the word, who hold the force, who are part of the Godhead, the magnificent Mother-Father Divine Self radiation. This is unmanifested glory and the opposite polarities and perfect balance and perfect expression of impulse by which each thing is derived. . . .

"Whereby each man, who is a spiritual son of the Godhead, is created out of the word of one of the seven aspects, he must serve upon that aspect or flame. You call them the rays of life. When a son or individuality is created under the auspices of the elohim, any one of these flames, you are pledged eternally unto that source and under that supervision. . . . These flames of life are as essential to your existence as your realization as a spiritual being, a son, a part of God."

It behooves us all to acknowledge the source of our life and to determine under which ray of life we have our existence.

Leo Tolstoy, the great Russian writer, was overwhelmed originally by the thought of his eventual death. Before his transformation to *homo religiosus* through Christianity, he wrote: "Sooner or later my affairs, whatever they may be, will be forgotten, and I shall not exist. Then why go on making any effort?"

This is Archangel Michael's answer to that question, given through me on October 19, 1971: "In the refinement of every form, of every source of Creative Energy life, a triune purpose exists: to be, to know and to act. As this is the fundamental principle of Life Force Itself, then no form you recognize, be it a stone or a man or an angel, can ever end his being, knowing and acting out. Regardless of what is thought by you now, it is possible to think beyond, to know beyond and to act beyond that which you have at your command and as part of your resources in the present time."

Let there be in every mind and every heart the comfort of the realization that there is a purpose for existing. This purpose is triune because Spirit—indeed, all life—is patterned after a trinity. Man has conceived of the Holy Trinity in many different ways. But in Its pure, ideal form, God or Spirit is life, light and love. Life, to be. Light, to know. Love, to act.

My Nada Self described it in a communication on June 26, 1966: "It must be understood positively by all men . . . that they are creative beings; that they have been created by the being nature of a God Force which is life itself; and that life is precious and must be expressed through love; and this love may have its energy and its total participation through enlightenment, which is the light side of the trinity."

Not only do we have a physical, genetic "book of life"; we have a spiritual book of life, as well, that is tangible to our psychic senses. This book or scroll of life is mentioned in John's book of Revelation. It refers to seven initiations or stages of spiritual development.*

Lord Michael expressed how important is our knowledge of these initiations on May 27, 1967: "The scroll of life within each soul is emblazoned across his very psychic intunement, for truth, light, love and personal contribution unto the record of mankind's evolvement. Each of you is part of that scroll. Within that scroll is your own personal light-form participation in the program. You have been given know-how unto this scroll of life. You have been given permission on opening it to conscious, mortal scriptures. You have been instructed to use it and to follow it. Your most important mission in life, here or elsewhere, is the following of the entire script within your personal unfoldment. . . .

"You have within you, each and every soul of creation, each child of God, the entire mystery of life enshrined, inscribed within the being of your creation. These are the so-called seven seals within the mind, the soul and the body of each being. These are covered by each soul in the proper prescribed manner as the soul takes on experience and life wherever he is guided to be given proper instruction for further development. It is part of the testing and pattern of life and evolvement and incarnation.

"Whether one incarnates here or elsewhere, each one of these centers is enshrined by the higher Self and the guardians of the area in which he or she takes upon himself a life potential; an incarnation, so to speak. Then he is given whatever tests, trials and tribulations are for his own purpose and ongoing. He is given these symbols and these intunements in order for him to overcome them, according to divine law and according to his own karmic pattern. . . .

"According to how deeply, how sincerely and how hard the

---

* See Mark-Age course *Seven Steps to Christhood*, by Robert H. Knapp, M.D.

application is put into practice, that is how much of that secret in-tunement is unveiled to the consciousness and used by the consciousness for his own advancement as a soul in the particular place where he may endeavor to grow and to open his book of life, so to speak."

Lord Michael reveals two enduring elements that are a part of our life journey. One, we need to live according to divine law. Two, we need to do so according to our own unique, individual karmic pattern. These are the same two elements that were clearly revealed by Jesus when he spoke to the rich young man about entering into spiritual life.

The man had asked Jesus what he should do to achieve eternal life. Jesus replied, "Obey the commandments." The man then asked, "Which ones?" Jesus answered: " 'Do not murder, do not commit adultery, do not steal, do not give false testimony, honor your father and mother,' and 'love your neighbor as yourself.' " These comprise the first element described by Lord Michael about living according to divine law.

The second element followed next in Jesus' exchange with the young man, as recorded in the Gospel of Matthew: "The young man said to him, 'I have obeyed all these from my boyhood; what do I lack?' Jesus said to him, 'If you wish to be perfect, go and sell your possessions and give them to the poor, and you will have a treasure in heaven; then follow me.' "

This exchange is equivalent to a modern-day soul reading. Jesus followed the same basic instruction Archangel Michael has given us, about following the script within our individual spiritual unfoldment, according to our own karmic history. Viewing this man's soul record from a Christ-conscious level, Jesus recommended a course of action whereby the rich young man would best be able to advance as a soul evolving within his own cause-and-effect pattern of life.

A divine echo reverberated within John Donne, English poet (1572–1631), when he penned these thoughts about the book of life immortal: "All mankind is of one Author, and is one volume; when one man dies, one chapter is not torn out of the book, but translated

into a better language; and every chapter must be so translated; . . .
but God's hand is in every translation, and His hand shall bind up
all our scattered leaves again for that library where every book shall
lie open to one another."

PERFECTION

Clear language is a hallmark of the channeled communications
through me which we have used to extract these twenty-three
cosmic laws. An example is this April 6, 1960, communication that
verifies the law of perfection. Zolanda, a member of the White
Brotherhood, explained: "Man evolves in cycles. Man is more than
a race. Man is a creation of divine thinking, which evolves until it
again becomes that original thought, pure and substance only. . . .
Man constantly is changing into a higher realm of being. Man shall
not cease evolving until each man . . . shall become as pure as the
original thought, which knows only the law of perfection."

The spiritual Hierarchy's message that God created man and all
other things perfect, and that man created his own imperfection but
retains his ability to become perfect again, has been transmitted to
and recorded by all the world's religions. Here are a few examples:

In Islam, the Sufis have the concept of the Perfect Human Being
who is any man, Muslim or otherwise, "who has fully realized his
essential oneness with the Divine Being in whose likeness he is
made."

In Buddhism, *paramitas,* which is Sanskrit for "perfections," are a
set of virtues strived for in order to reintegrate with the transcendent
absolute.

In Hinduism, ultimate reality is perfection. Man is perfectible
because atman, the human spirit, is inseparable from Brahman, the
perfect Absolute.

The Musar school, a Jewish meditative movement begun in the

1800s, teaches that perfecting oneself is an obligation.

Every denomination in Christianity has formulated its interpretation of Jesus' precise instruction to humanity, "Be perfect, therefore, as your heavenly Father is perfect."

Religions place so much importance on the notion of man's ability to progress and return to perfection in Spirit that Swedish theologian Anders Nygren states: "A religion which did not claim to make possible the meeting between the eternal and man, a religion which did not claim to be the bridge over an otherwise impassable gulf, would be a monstrosity."

One valid reason it would be monstrous not to acknowledge perfection as a divine principle which can be lived was communicated by Sananda on April 22, 1973: "That which is based on error or misconception or conceit or ego has its day, but loses its impetus in time; and by the divine law of God cannot exist, for it . . . has destroyed more than it has enhanced. By this divine law of truth and eternal perfection, it cannot exist."

Here, then, is the universal principle which ensures that what is evil in our lives and in the world is only temporary. Error can never be permanent. Only those acts of man which are righteous can survive and can contribute to a stable, finished form.

Also, this law rules out eternal damnation since no one can remain eternally in error. The law of perfection convinces us that there is always hope. We can have faith that all actions in concord with spiritual principles will work towards a final perfect outcome. What could possibly be a more positive message?

Let us look within ourselves and examine what this law means to us and how we personally are to express it. The last thing we want to do is reject a principle of God.

On June 12, 1962, Sananda relayed how much the Hierarchy values this law: "Absolute correction means any disharmonious conditions are to be found, eliminated and replaced. We refuse to work outside of a perfect plan for a perfect planet under a perfect God consciousness. Everything we have ever attempted is to bring about this perfection in time, in space, in energy. Discuss whatever you need to discuss about . . . problems. But betray us not by thinking anything but the plan of perfection is absolutely mandatory."

In the deepest part of our being, none of us ever wishes to betray our Father-Mother Creator. Then how do we live the law of perfection? How are we to live all of the laws of Spirit perfectly? We may think that this law demands perfection immediately. Some psychological and metaphysical teachings claim that all is already perfect, that everything that happens to us individually and collectively is perfect because there is a perfect reason for it. By this logic every experience, good or bad, is somehow perfect. This supposedly explains God's perfection.

But our mortal will is only perfect when it is in harmony with Spirit's will. If it is not, there is imperfection. Therefore, not everything is perfect simply as it is. The dictionary confirms this; one meaning of *perfection* is "the act or process of perfecting." Obviously, something that needs perfecting is not perfect.

Perfection is a process that involves many steps and takes time. The law of growth and evolution, for example, demonstrates what perfection means. Under this law, trial and *error* are permissible in our physical, mental, emotional and spiritual development. We can make honest mistakes and still be within the law. This is true of our quest to understand and to act in conformance with every universal law. Therefore, we do not have to be perfect to be in harmony with the law of perfection.

How long should the perfecting of self take? What time frame should we envision? The Hierarchy has indicated that no one will be able to demonstrate fully the transmutation of the four lower bodies —mental, emotional, physical and soul—into the spiritual or light body before the Second Coming, which is expected in the beginning decades of the new millennium. In fact, it will take thousands of years to perfect all things on Earth; that is, to transform all conditions here into fourth dimensional, spiritual purity. So, let us have a realistic time frame.

Many notable religious leaders, East and West, have claimed that God's grace alone, not man's actions, can save him and bring him into perfection. For example, Christian theologians Martin Luther and John Calvin preached that neither man's free will, nor his love, nor any other human quality can lead to his perfection. Only God's grace can save him. In Japan, similar ideas about grace were taught by Honen and Shinran of the Pure Land sect of Mahayana Buddhism.

But one component of Spirit's grace is Its gift of free will to man. Consequently, we each are obligated to exercise our free will to erase all that is undesirable within us and in the world.

The Hasidim of Judaism teach that although the laws of God, which they number at 613, must be absolutely adhered to at all times, unnecessary strictness in observing those laws also must be avoided. Rabbi Nachman of Breslov explains: "Serve God with simplicity, without sophistication and hairsplitting. . . . You should not be overly strict and stringent, as it is written, '[Keep My decrees and laws, for if a man does them] he shall live by them' (Leviticus 18:4). [Our sages comment,] 'live by them—and do not die by them.' "

In a humorous yet serious way, Rabbi Nachman and the sages taught that perfection is a process that takes time. It requires flexibility as well as vigilance; otherwise, we defeat the very purpose of this law. For how can we become perfect if we kill ourselves trying?

In a December 26, 1962, communication, Sananda-Jesus exhorts us to be compassionate towards one another as we refine ourselves: "You have found many errors, dense and diseased parts of your own thinking, your own beliefs and your own conceptions. In this case you have removed them. . . .

"However, you also have known that many are encrusted with ideas and beliefs that are not easily removed, any more easily removed than parts of your own thoughts and conditions of life. How can we then condemn or hurt another? . . . He who is flawless is not in any kingdom, to my knowledge; for all have perfection yet ahead. All who seek perfection find higher evolvements to work into. Therefore, none can be the least satisfied with his status quo or present condition. . . .

"Nothing, then, is completed. No man is finished where he is. Therefore, I implore you, one and all, to seek the mercy you desire for your own light's experience. None who is sincere would wish to be condemned for seeking further proof, further understanding and further love demonstrations. . . . I ask, therefore, all who hear and who will understand, for more mercy unto his brother and sister on Earth, and in other levels and dimensions connected and coordinated with the Earth planet."

Perfection also is defined as "a person or thing that is the perfect embodiment of some quality." The word *quality* is singular and that is what the Hierarchy usually means when referring to perfection. In other words, our soul mission for any given lifetime may be only to perfect one talent or at most to work on a few. We need not burden ourselves thinking that we have to develop and to perfect every single quality or talent that we lack.

In one communication, Lord Maitreya gave the example of Sananda's incarnations as Gautama Buddha and as Jesus. In the incarnation of Gautama Buddha, he perfected within himself the understanding of God and the attunement with God consciousness. As Jesus, he discovered and perfected the love for God and for all other creatures.

To be true to our soul mission, we must be clear about what faculties or talents we are to perfect in this incarnation. We cannot be everything to everybody. Only God can. We need not take on too much. We also must guard against working on talents already perfected. As John Mark channeled on June 30, 1962, "Would you want two livers in the same body, and no heart? Of course not. Nor would the Christ or Spirit which is all-wise duplicate Itself, for this would not serve Its end purpose of perfection."

Who has not felt peer pressure—in school, society and the workplace—not to make mistakes; which is virtually the same thing as insisting that a person be perfect regardless of circumstances? Who has not been ridiculed or felt embarrassed as a child or as an adult when making a mistake? Let us not cave in to these pressures by doing only those things which we already have mastered rather than developing other faculties where we are less adept and may be more vulnerable.

The *Bhagavad Gita* states: "By devotion to one's own particular duty, everyone can attain perfection. Let me tell you how. By performing his own work, one worships the Creator who dwells in every creature. Such worship brings that person to fulfillment. It is better to perform one's own duties imperfectly than to master the duties of another. By fulfilling the obligations he is born with, a person never comes to grief. No one should abandon duties because he sees defects in them. Every action, every activity, is surrounded by defects as a fire is surrounded by smoke."

Let us take courage and perfect what Spirit would have us perfect. God knows our soul mission, and what duties are before us to perfect, better than we do.

Here is another valuable lesson in evaluating how far we have progressed in the perfecting of a talent or a quality. We may not express perfectly now what we already have mastered in prior incarnations. Sananda explains in this April 30, 1961, communication:

"Developing [a talent, a faculty or a virtue] may take eons of time and incarnations, perhaps confining all of those to one galaxy, or even one planet, until it became perfected. The soul or spirit then perhaps would concentrate on another facet. . . . This may take the spirit or the soul into an entirely different set of conditions, vibrations or manifestations. You would not be thinking of the first set of conditions, and might not even be aware that they were stored up within the soul or spiritual records of that individualization of spiritual energy, that particular being. But when you put all the facets together, you would then have a creation of God that was equal to the role of a child of God, a true cocreator."

We may not know about qualities we ourselves have perfected, and have even less knowledge about perfected traits in others. This is another reason for being merciful and compassionate in our evaluation of our own and others' spiritual evolution.

On January 14, 1961, John Mark channeled a description of what spiritual perfection entails: "Liken it unto Jesus of Nazareth when he walked in that life. When his mission was revealed to him, there could not be in his mind anywhere the doubt of his subconscious,

138

the fear of conscious activity nor of the intunement of his supercon-scious Self. He was perfection incarnate in that he realized the Source and the role of his subconscious. He was fearless and bold and loving and tender, demanding and forceful in his conscious action. He was completely subservient to the will of his supercon-scious, Christ Self."

Imperfect as we are, do we have a clear starting point by which we may begin the process of perfection? Yes. On May 3, 1961, Jesus instructed us simply to call on the divine perfection that already is implanted within us:

"The way to restore the divine pattern is by dwelling on the divine pattern, by knowing in your heart and feeling most earnestly that that divine pattern is your natural heritage. This would apply to want on the physical, supply or substance. This would apply to health, the pattern you are expressing in your body. It would apply to all your relationships with life, whether it be other people or . . . the harmony you would feel in life itself, in your expression itself.

"It is true that the true child of God lives in a paradise or an Eden. In order to manifest that condition of perfection, one must recognize that he or she is truly a child of God and all is perfect in that image.

"In Spirit all is perfect. All is powerful. Therefore, as a true child of God, when he or she would see disharmony or be in disharmony, all that a true child would do would be to ask that it be restored. According to the faith that one would feel for this truth, that is how quickly this harmony would be restored. In other words, if one had the faith instantly that this was one's true state of being, instantly it would be restored. If the faith was weak and he or she needed proof and was insecure in this understanding, it would take a little time to work through one's own consciousness and manifest on or in one's own expression or life. . . .

"In all my ministry as Jesus of Nazareth, there was only one state of consciousness I was able to demonstrate. That was my divine right to be as a cocreator with God, a son of God, which gave me equal rights with His-Her perfection."

Each of us has equal rights in God's perfection. Yet, we seem to know more about how imperfect we are rather than how perfect we are. Shouldn't we spend at least as much time knowing our divine perfection as our mortal imperfections?

In a spring 1991 meditation, a friend who suffered from a medical condition received for her own healing the very words Sananda-Jesus had expressed thirty years previously. "Three days ago," she wrote, "I had the most profound meditation I have ever had. The words came for me to declare, 'It is my inherent divine right as a child of God to have perfect health.' The beautiful image came to me of a golden column or rod coming down through my head. . . . Gold light poured outward and upward from me. My physical body began to dissolve and the reality of my being was visible to me. This pure light looked alien to me and was the most wonderful thing I have ever seen."

Oneness with God's perfection need not feel alien to us. Inevitably we must accept this and every other cosmic law. In Spirit we are perfect. To know this perfection, we must experience perfection. Only then can we affirm the perfection of others. This is how we love God and love one another, perfectly.

My Nada Self channeled on October 31, 1962: "You may not know me, and I may not know you. . . . I may not know how you serve. You may be unto me a stranger in some distant field, and I may be unto you no name and no conscious connection.

"Nevertheless, in Spirit and in the Christ, all become united. One, we serve! One body of light, one energy of force, we serve our Father-Mother God. For we are the Son, and as the Son we cannot be separated. Every particle of the Sonship is a part of a body that is whole. As Christ Jesus demonstrated, God cannot see error, confusion or disease in the body of another individual. God cannot see error in His-Her Son, which is mankind. He-She sees only the wholeness of each cell, and each soul joined together and aligned in perfect harmony and balance.

"Therefore, with this concentration of the light and love of our Father-Mother God, we are drawn together and become a whole aspect, a whole demonstration, a whole race returning in perfection, in love and in service; being one with one another, thereby loving one another, showing and demonstrating the love of God, who created us one, one, one."

Be therefore perfect, even as our Father in heaven is perfect.

KEEP MY COMMANDMENTS

In our journey to higher consciousness it is absolutely vital to remember that divine laws interact together as a whole. The basis for this divine integrity is Spirit's universal laws of oneness and integration. One of God's most holy manifestations of unity is: every single cosmic law includes every other cosmic law. Divine Mind conceives perfectly.

In his book *The Light Beyond*, Rabbi Kaplan quotes the great sage and founder of Hasidism, the Baal Shem Tov, on the mystery of God's oneness: "Whenever we grasp hold of any part of this unity, we grasp it all. This is true even when one grasps its outermost 'edge.' "

God's integrated laws acting as one divine power is apparent in Jesus' direction to his disciples, "If you love me, keep my commandments." Simply and precisely expressing one divine law, in this instance love, requires keeping all divine statutes.

The term *unconditional*, as in the phrase "unconditional love," is applied to every cosmic law. Spirit expresses unconditional love and order, unconditional equality and individuality, unconditional life, and so on. Spirit, being Its own laws, expresses Its will and creative life force unconditionally and perfectly.

What makes an act of love, or an act of any other divine law, unconditional? God's oneness and integration. Love becomes unconditional when all of the conditions for divine love are met. The conditions of love are the inclusion and the enactment of all the other principles of God. When all the laws of God are integrated into an act of love, love is unconditional. Whenever even one of God's laws is forgotten and left out of the equation, love becomes conditional–because there still is an aspect of love to be fulfilled before genuine love is achieved.

Unconditionality is true of every divine law. God's love differs from man's because His omniscience provides a perfect awareness of the oneness of all life, energies and principles, and of the requirement to express as an integrated, interrelated whole.

Great Learning, a Confucian document, beautifully expresses God's unified principles affecting every level of human interaction:

"The ancients who wished to manifest their clear character to the world would first bring order to their states. Those who wished to bring order to their states would first regulate their families. Those who wished to regulate their families would first cultivate their personal lives. Those who wished to cultivate their personal lives would first rectify their minds. Those who wished to rectify their minds would first make their wills sincere. Those who wished to make their wills sincere would first extend their knowledge.

"The extension of knowledge consists in the investigation of things. When things are investigated, knowledge is extended; when knowledge is extended, the will becomes sincere; when the will is sincere, the mind is rectified; when the mind is rectified, the personal life is cultivated; when the personal life is cultivated, the family will be regulated; when the family is regulated, the state will be in order; and when the state is in order, there will be peace throughout the world. From the Son of Heaven down to the common people, all must regard cultivation of the personal life as the root or foundation. There is never a case when the root is in disorder and yet the branches are in order."

The "center of the hourglass," so-called, makes this text remarkable. The locus upon which all of these interconnecting, interdependent conditions of human life hinge is the "investigation of things."

What are these things? Chu Hsi* remarked: "The meaning of the expression 'The perfection of knowledge depends on the investigation of things (ko-wu)' is this: If we wish to extend our knowledge to the utmost, we must investigate the principles of all things we come into contact with. . . . It is only because all principles are not investigated that man's knowledge is incomplete."

Expressed in another way: perfect understanding of principles or cosmic laws is the surest way to rectify the mind, the family, the society and the nation, and to bring about world peace. Rectification begins in consciousness. Change in our consciousness invariably leads to change in our personal lives.

As the *Great Learning* teaches, "There is never a case when the root [consciousness] is in disorder and yet the branches [outward manifestations of consciousness] are in order." Hence, never is there a situation in which we imperfectly understand spiritual principles and yet have perfect order in our personal lives and in the world.

Knowledge of cosmic laws, however, will not fully bring us into enlightenment. We have to take that next important step: using those laws. Only then can we witness the true power of Almighty God in our lives and in the transformation of this world.

"It is now the present," begins Glo-Ria, in a communication on August 13, 1963, "and the era of the present says that we are about to bring into manifestation a higher principle of life, a more conscious awareness of God's divine laws in motion, in every aspect of Earth's life. This includes political government, it includes economic freedom, it includes the freedom to express and to explore the individual Self in every field of life, understanding, education, recreation, being and comfort.

"How can we do this? Only by consciously understanding the

---

* Chu Hsi (1130–1200) was one of China's five greatest philosophers, along with Confucius, Mencius, Lao Tzu and Chuang Tzu. He combined four classics of Chinese philosophy—the *Analects* of Confucius, the *Book of Mencius,* the *Great Learning,* and the *Doctrine of the Mean*—into one grouping, the *Four Books,* with his commentary. From 1313 to 1905 the *Four Books* were the basis for civil service examinations. Thus, for over six hundred years his work exercised greater influence than any other system of thought.

divine laws that are at work in the universe, and *using them.* I have used the words *application* and *apply* over and over again, because it is of no avail unless you learn to apply what you know. It is all well and good to have all this knowledge; you can go through college and study all the fine principles and the greatest of formulas, but if you do not go out and apply them and make a better world, what good is all that knowledge?

"So it has been with man on the Earth for thousands and thousands of years. As a matter of fact, the whole . . . project of education for the race karma on Earth has been to teach man finally to apply what he knows, in the right and positive side of the ledger instead of the negative side of the ledger.

"In ancient lands and histories and civilizations known as Lemuria and Atlantis, man had this knowledge, as he has this knowledge right here today on Earth. But he applied these things on the negative side of the ledger, and many destructive and ugly conditions were allowed to exist. But this was man's growth. He did learn how to use and to apply God's laws and the material substance which we call frequency vibration in motion.

"Now man must swing the pendulum to the other side of the road. That side is to bring about a positive, gracious, good, fine life of productivity for equal means that all will be welcome to use. Yes, this means all, everyone on Earth must be conscious of his divine heritage as a child of God. Every single soul on the Earth must begin to use material of the spiritual substance in manipulating a better life for his own individual life and for the life of the group with which he is involved.

"Remember, we use the word *group* often to mean just a family circle, often to mean a small community, but certainly to mean the whole Earth planet, the world as we are concerned with it here and now. So be about our Father's business and start learning this manipulation of matter."

EPILOGUE

ACCEPT GOD

"All good things must end." However, where eternal principles of God are concerned, this phrase can never apply. Forever we shall be involved with the universal laws of life. As we strive for a better understanding of God and for a more perfect life, continually we will gain new and more profound insights into the First Cause, the Good, the Old One, Principle Itself, our Father-Mother God. The quest for spiritual principles is never-ending; our divine journey always is beginning anew. The cosmos holds new laws yet to be discovered.

Let us inquire into one final mystery. Why did not the Hierarchy, those who represent the spiritual government of our solar system and who currently are guiding the spiritual upliftment of planet Earth into the fourth dimension, give Mark and me, cofounders of Mark-Age, a simple and complete list of the spiritual laws of the universe? What could be more helpful to people's spiritual development, in order to ensure the success of the Second Coming of Sananda-Jesus, Prince of Earth, and simultaneously the second coming of our own Christ Self? What could be more logical than for us to receive these commandments at the start of our partnership and our special work together?

Through the centuries, Jewish sages puzzled over a similar question. They asked themselves why the Ten Commandments were not at the very beginning of the Torah. Why did not God reveal the laws to Abraham, Isaac or Jacob? Why did the Ten Commandments have to wait until Moses' time?

Likewise, we should ask why a complete listing of cosmic laws was not given at the inception of every major philosophy and religion. We could ask ourselves about our own spiritual awakening.

Did God, through our individualized I Am Self, reveal fully all of the universal, spiritual principles of the cosmos as well as a complete understanding of them? There is no record in history of anyone being so fully informed by his or her Christ Self–be he or she a common person or a founder of a major religion or philosophy.

How is this possible? We all realize that to know God is to love God. In loving God, we are able to love one another wonderfully, completely, righteously and unconditionally. This is our goal as children of God. This is what each life form, in the deepest part of its being, yearns to be, to know and to do. Why is it, then, that we do not have clear knowledge of God's laws from the moment we awaken and desire to do His-Her will more than ever before in our lives?

Ephraim Urbach, a professor of Talmud, discloses the answer in his book *The Sages: Their Concepts and Beliefs:* "The very question 'Why were the Ten Commandments not cited at the beginning of the Torah?' flows from the view that the whole concern of the Torah is the precept, and that the entire election of Israel took place only that the Torah might be accepted. All that preceded–the history of the Patriarchs, the bondage of Egypt and the Exodus–is not of primary importance. All these are to be understood as preparatory events leading to the Revelation [the receiving of the Ten Commandments]."

Only when we are able to accept God's laws will they be revealed to us. Divine principles govern the spiritual awakening process just as they govern every other aspect of life. Cosmic laws, such as growth and evolution, and love, protect us from inadvertently resisting or rejecting spiritual principles before we can accept and understand them enough to use them wisely.

Do not resort to self-criticism or a sense of inferiority. Do not think that the reason you cannot clearly receive the laws, or gain insight into specific laws in response to your prayers and meditations, might be that you are not advanced enough, or not capable enough, or not good enough.

Replace these debilitating attitudes with the truth. As children of

God, all of us do, either consciously or unconsciously, receive Spirit daily. Our very existence is proof that each of us accepts God as Divine Creative Energy and God as the Spiritual Principle that governs that Energy. Actually, we have been accepting and acknowledging God ever since we were created.

Mary and Jesus did not create a new pattern when they demonstrated the immaculate conception and virgin birth. They were following the pattern set by our Father-Mother God in creating each one of us. Throughout creation the race of man was conceived and created immaculate. Where Emmanuel (God within us) resides, we each are perfectly clean, without spot; perfectly correct, without flaw, fault or error; pure, innocent and without sin. Therefore, since no child of Spirit ever can be completely separate from his or her Creator, it follows that whoever is alive accepts God.

As we serve God, humanity and all life, we dare not deny this truth. We neither judge nor cast aside one lost sheep, to use Jesus' analogy, because we know that each and every person, to some degree, accepts the laws and the energy of our common Creator.

Humankind in every culture—whether theistic or atheistic, gnostic or agnostic, deistic or moralistic—has received God's revelation of cosmic laws throughout history. The presence of God within us renders the labels we attach to our thought-systems meaningless. Only what is in the mind, the heart, the soul and the physical acts of man has true value.

Before Hinduism, peoples of the Indian subcontinent received God's laws as *rita*. Afterwards, along with the creation of Buddhism, the laws of God were conceived of as *dharma*. To Egyptians, spiritual laws were known as *maat;* to Greeks, *logos;* to Chinese and other Asian peoples, *li, tao, t'ien-ming;* to Romans, *dike* (natural law); to the Islamic world, *shari'ah.* Every native culture around the world has its own name for the inescapable principles of life.

The apostle Paul found this out in his missionary journeys, as did other Christian missionaries—often to their surprise—in their travels to spread the gospel to other parts of the world. Paul referred to this prior knowledge in his epistle to the Romans: "Indeed, when Gentiles, who do not have the law, do by nature things required by the law, they are a law for themselves, even though they do not have the law, since they show that the requirements of the law are written on their hearts."

Well, it also was written in their books. Before Jesus and Paul, there was Cicero, a Roman statesman and philosopher of the first century before Christ and the author of one of the finest formulations of cosmic law ever written.

Cicero wrote: "True law is right reason in agreement with nature; it is of universal application, unchanging and everlasting; it summons to duty by its commands, and averts from wrongdoing by its prohibitions. . . . It is wrong to alter this law or to repeal any part of it, and it is impossible to abolish it completely. Neither senate nor people can free us from its obligation, and we need no one outside ourselves to expound or interpret it. It does not ordain different laws for Rome and Athens, for now and in the future, but one eternal and unchangeable law valid for all nations and all times, and there will be one common teacher and ruler over us, God, author of this law, interpreter, and enforcer."

No wonder Paul would explain that certain people had the law of God "written on their hearts."

By focusing solely on man's trials and tribulations, we might be tempted to conclude that we, as a race, are not working with or countenancing cosmic laws. Instead, let us trace briefly the lineage and legacy of one cosmic law, love, through the religious and philosophical traditions of Western civilization.

The following is only one of the innumerable paths we could track. For as J. Bruce Long writes in the opening of his article on "Love" in *The Encyclopedia of Religion*, "The concept of love, in one form or another, has informed the definition and development of almost every human culture in the history of the world—past and present, East and West, primitive and complex."

The idea of love originated in Divine Mind. But let our starting point for love as a divine law of God be the revelations of Moses. In the Ten Commandments it is written, "I am the Lord your God,

. . . showing mercy to thousands of generations of those who love Me and keep My commandments."

Jumping ahead many centuries, to the Golden Age of Greece, we find that the race of man acquired powerful conceptions of love through the teachings of three directors of the spiritual Hierarchy: Sananda in his incarnation as Socrates, Hilarion as Plato, and Kut Humi as Aristotle.

Further on, Sananda, in his incarnation as Jesus, focused attention on love by teaching that it was the greatest of all commandments. Centuries later, Thomas Aquinas, the renowned thirteenth-century Catholic theologian, reinvigorated thinking about this divine law by fusing Jesus' teachings about love with those of Aristotle.

In the late 1500s through the mid-1600s, Francisco Suárez of Spain, a Catholic Thomist and the greatest of all Jesuit theologians, identified the natural precept of mutual love as the power that directs man's society, his political institutions and relations between nations. Suárez, along with a Protestant Dutch contemporary, Hugo Grotius, founder of modern natural law theory, linked love and natural law together as the foundation of what later became international law.

Out of this tradition, in the late 1700s, a new nation was born. Thomas Jefferson, James Madison, George Mason, Samuel and John Adams, Benjamin Franklin and the other Founding Fathers created the United States of America. From this same tradition also came international organizations such as the United Nations and particularly its 1948 document, the Universal Declaration of Human Rights.

A product of this legacy of love is a coworker in the spiritual plan and program for Earth and a friend of Mark-Age, Robert Muller, former United Nations Assistant Secretary-General. He brings this divine lineage of love full circle with this realization, from his book *New Genesis: Shaping a Global Spirituality:*

"I have come to believe firmly today that our future peace, justice, fulfillment, happiness and harmony on this planet will not depend on world government but on divine or cosmic government, meaning that we must seek and apply the 'natural,' 'evolutionary,' 'divine,' 'universal' or 'cosmic' laws which must rule our journey in the cosmos. Most of these laws can be found in the great religions and prophecies, and they are being rediscovered slowly but surely in the world organizations."

Let us keep this legacy alive by becoming divine law in action. Let us pray that everyone everywhere accept and live in concord with cosmic laws. In doing so, we help ourselves and our sisters and brothers fulfill God's prophecy to Jeremiah concerning the Latter Days before the coming of the Messiah: "This is the covenant I will make . . . , declares the Lord. I will put My law in their minds and write it on their hearts."

FOLLOW GOD'S LAWS

How then does one come into this awareness of God within and God around him? By following the laws God has laid down for man to follow. How did these laws come to be given to man? Through the powers of Almighty God and the recognition of certain of His sons of the God power within themselves. These are your prophets, your sages, your wise men and your saints. These sons, who are your brothers, have learned and have sent the message out to the world to recognize and to follow. It is all written, but each generation needs to have it restated for them.

In just that way you as an individual must restate God's laws and follow them daily in your life. We tell you to pray continuously, to meditate on God's laws and commandments. We tell you to follow our instructions every day, every moment of every day. Why do we say this? Because it is necessary to restate, to remind, to reactivate these fundamental laws of God.

They will operate without your restatement and reevaluation, but you cannot function without regenerating what you are. What you are is what you think and what you believe. Therefore, by restating every moment of every day who you are, what you believe, and how you think of God, you are rebuilding, regenerating, reestablishing your inner Self, your spiritual Self; which rules, governs and determines the health of your mind, body and your soul. As you think, so you are.

— *Paul the Apostle; March 25, 1958*

BIBLIOGRAPHY

Aristotle. "Metaphysics." *A New Aristotle Reader.* Ed. J. L. Ackrill. Trans. W. E. Ross. Princeton, N.J.: Princeton University Press, 1987.

Byrom, Thomas, trans. *The Dhammapada.* New York: Vintage Books, 1976.

Chan, Wing-tsit, trans. and ed. *A Source Book in Chinese Philosophy.* Princeton, N.J.: Princeton University Press, 1963.

Easwaran, Eknath, trans. *The Bhagavad Gita.* Petaluma, Calif.: Nilgiri Press, 1985.

Easwaran, Eknath, trans. *The Dhammapada.* Petaluma, Calif.: Nilgiri Press, 1986.

Easwaran, Eknath, trans. *The Upanishads.* Petaluma, Calif.: Nilgiri Press, 1987.

Eliade, Mircea, ed. *The Encyclopedia of Religion.* New York: Macmillan Publishing Company, 1987.

Eliade, Mircea. *A History of Religious Ideas.* 3 vols. Trans. Willard R. Trask, Alf Hiltebeitel and Diane Apostolos-Cappadona. Chicago: The University of Chicago Press, 1978.

Gandhi, Mahatma. *All Men Are Brothers.* New York: The Continuum Publishing Corporation, 1980.

Head, Joseph, and S. L. Cranston, eds. *Reincarnation: The Phoenix Fire Mystery.* New York: Julian Press-Crown Publishers, Inc., 1977.

Kaplan, Aryeh. *Jewish Meditation: A Practical Guide.* New York: Schocken Books, 1985.

Kaplan, Aryeh. *The Light Beyond: Adventures in Hassidic Thought.* New York: Maznaim Publishing Corporation, 1981.

Lamsa, George M. *Old Testament Light.* Philadelphia: A. J. Holman Company, 1978.

Lao Tzu. *Lao tzu / Tao te ching.* Trans. D. C. Lau. Harmondsworth, Middlesex, England: Penguin Books, 1985.

Lao Tzu. *Tao te ching.* Trans. Gia-fu Feng and Jane English. New York: Vintage Books, 1972.

Muller, Robert. *New Genesis: Shaping a Global Spirituality*. Garden City, N.Y.: Doubleday & Company, Inc., 1982.

Plato. "Phaedo." *The Dialogues of Plato*. Trans. R. S. Bluck. New York: Bantam Books, 1986.

Plaut, W. Gunther, ed. *The Torah: A Modern Commentary*. New York: The Union of American Hebrew Congregations, 1981.

Rahula, Walpola. *What the Buddha Taught*. New York: Grove Press, Inc., 1974.

Urbach, Ephraim E. *The Sages: Their Concepts and Beliefs*. Trans. Israel Abrahams. Cambridge, Mass.: Harvard University Press, 1975.

GLOSSARY

Abel: son of Adam and Eve, in biblical allegory; was not a person. Abel and Cain were the two clans of the Adamic race within the Elder race on Earth prior to Lemuria. The Abels wished to help raise their fallen brothers of the human subrace back into the fourth dimension. The Cains wanted to keep the humans in the third dimension as subjects.

akashic record: soul history of an individual, a race, a heavenly body.

angel: a being of celestial realms. Angels manage, direct and cocreate with God the forms that exist in all space and eternity. They are a separate kingdom from man, and cannot incarnate physically.

Aquarian Age: period of approximately two thousand years following the Piscean Age, beginning around A.D. 2000. Cycle during which the solar system moves through the area of cosmic space known as Aquarius.

archangel: head of a ray of life in this solar system. First: Michael. Second: Jophiel. Third: Chamuel (replaced Lucifer). Fourth: Gabriel. Fifth: Raphael. Sixth: Zadkiel. Seventh: Uriel (only one of feminine polarity).

Armageddon: the Latter-Day, cleansing, harvest, Mark Age period immediately prior to the Second Coming of Sananda as Christ Jesus. The era wherein man must eliminate the negativity in himself and the world.

ascended master: one who has reached the Christ level and who has translated his or her physical body into the light body or etheric body.

astral: pertaining to realms or planes between physical and etheric. Lower astral realms approximate Earth plane level of consciousness; higher astral realms approach etheric or Christ realms.

astral body: one of the seven bodies of man pertaining to Earth plane life. Appearance is similar to physical body. Upon transition called death it becomes the operative body for the consciousness, in the astral realms.

Atlantis: civilization springing from Lemuria, dating from 206,000 to 10,000 years ago. Land area was from present eastern USA and the Caribbean to western Europe, but not all one land mass. Sinking of Atlantis was from 26,000 to 10,000 years ago; allegory of Noah and the Flood.

aura: the force field around a person or an object. Contains information graphically revealed in color to those able to see with spiritual vision.

bilocation: being in more than one place at the same time.

Cain: son of Adam and Eve, in biblical allegory; was not a person. See *Abel.*

153

chakra: a center of energy focus, located around one of the seven major endocrine glands, but which penetrates the other, more subtle, bodies.

channel: a person who is used to transmit communications, energies, thoughts, deeds by either Spirit or an agent of Spirit. Also called prophet, sensitive, recorder, medium, instrument.

chohans: directors of the Seven Rays of Life, under the archangels. First: El Morya. Second: Kut Humi. Third: Lanto. Fourth: Serapis Bey. Fifth: Hilarion. Sixth: St. Germain. Seventh: Sananda with Nada. As channeled through Yolanda numerous times.

Christ: a title indicating achievement of the spiritual consciousness of a son of God. Also refers to the entire race of man as and when operating in that level of consciousness.

Christ, anti-: one who does not accept brotherhood and equality of all men as sons of God.

Christ awareness: awareness of the Christ level within one's self and of the potential to achieve such.

Christ consciousness: achievement of some degree of understanding and use of spiritual powers and talents.

Christ Self: the superconscious, I Am, higher Self, oversoul level of consciousness.

conscious mind: the mortal level of one's total consciousness; which is about one tenth of such total consciousness. Usually refers to the rational, thinking aspect in man.

consciousness, mass: collective consciousness of race of man on Earth, all planes or realms pertaining to Earth.

Creative Energy: a designation for God or Spirit or Creative Force.

death: transition from physical life or expression on Earth to another realm, such as physical incarnation on some other planet or expression on astral or etheric realms.

dematerialize: change of rate of frequency vibration so as to disappear from third dimensional range of Earth plane sensing.

devas: those intelligent entities of the etheric planes who control the patterns for manifested form in the etheric, Earth and astral planes, under the direction of the angelic kingdom.

devic: one of the kingdoms of God's creation of entities. See *devas.*

dimension: a plane or realm of manifestation. A range of frequency vibration expression, such as third dimensional physical on Earth.

Divine Mind: God or Spirit; in reality the only mind that exists, man having a consciousness within this one mind.

elementals: those intelligent entities supervising the elements which comprise manifested form in the Earth and astral planes, under the direction of the devas for those forms.

154

elohim: one or more of the seven elohim in the Godhead, heading the Seven Rays of Life; creators of manifestation for Spirit.

emotional body: one of the seven bodies of man pertaining to Earth life. Does not in any way resemble the physical body, but has the connotation of a vehicle for expression.

ESP: elementary spiritual powers, the definition coined by Mark-Age in 1966 to supersede the limited and nonspiritual usual meaning as extrasensory perception.

etheric: the Christ realms. Interpenetrates the entire solar system, including the physical and astral realms.

etheric body: one of the seven bodies of man pertaining to Earth life. Known more commonly as the light body, the electric body, the resurrected body, the ascended body. Resembles the physical body, but not necessarily of the same appearance. This body can be used by the Christ Self for full expression of Christ talents and powers.

eye, third: the spiritual sight or vision. Spiritual focus of light in center of forehead.

fall of man: sons of God becoming entrapped in the third or physical dimension of Earth from 206,000,000 to 26,000,000 years ago.

Father-Mother God: indicates male-female or positive-negative principle and polarities of Spirit. Also, Father denotes action and ideation, while Mother symbolizes receptive principles.

Father-Mother-Son: the Holy Trinity wherein Father is originator of idea for manifestation, Mother (Holy Spirit or Holy Ghost) brings forth the idea into manifestation, Son is the manifestation. Son also denotes the Christ or the race of mankind, universally.

Federation of Planets: coordination and cooperation of man on all planets of this solar system, except as yet man of physical and astral realms of Earth.

forces, negative: individuals, groups or forces not spiritually enlightened or oriented, but who think and act in antispiritual manners.

fourth dimension: in spiritual sense, the next phase of Earthman's evolution into Christ awareness and use of ESP, elementary spiritual powers. In physical sense, the next higher frequency vibration range into which Earth is being transmuted.

free will: man's divine heritage to make his own decisions. Pertains fully only to the Christ Self; and only in part and for a limited, although often lengthy, period to the mortal self or consciousness during the soul evolvement.

frequency vibration: a range of energy expressing as matter. Present Earth understanding and measurement, as in cycles per second, not applicable.

Golden Age or Era: the incoming New Age or Aquarian Age, taking effect

155

fully with the return of Sananda early in the twenty-first century. It will be the age of greatest spiritual enlightenment in Earth's history.

heaven: an attitude and atmosphere of man's expression, wherever he is. No such specific place, as believed by some religions; except to denote the etheric realms.

hell: an attitude and atmosphere of man's expression, wherever he is. No such specific place, as believed by some religions.

Hierarchal Board: the spiritual governing body of this solar system. Headquarters is on Saturn.

hierarchal plan and program: the 26,000-year program ending around A.D. 2000 wherein the Hierarchal Board has been lifting man of Earth into Christ awareness preparatory to the manifestation of spiritual government on Earth and the return of Earth to the Federation of Planets of this solar system.

Hierarchy, spiritual: the spiritual government of the solar system, from the Hierarchal Board down through the individual planetary departments.

hieronics: higher plane electromagnetic energies transmitted from interdimensional spacecraft to assist transmutation of individuals and groups.

I Am: the Christ or high Self of each person. Yahweh (Jehovah), in the Old Testament. Atman or Brahman.

I Am Nation: spiritual government of, for and by the I Am Selves of all people on Earth, to be inaugurated officially by Sananda upon his Second Coming. Neither a religion nor a political government, it is the congregation of all souls dedicated, above any other allegiance, to God and to expressing the I Am Self. Regardless of race, gender, age, nationality, religion or esoteric group affiliation, everyone is a potential I Am Nation citizen. On May 10, 1974, the Hierarchal Board commissioned Mark-Age to implant the prototype of the I Am Nation.

incarnation: one lifetime of a soul; not always referring to an experience on Earth only.

Jesus of Nazareth: last Earth incarnation of Sananda. Christ Jesus, rather than Jesus Christ; for Christ is not a name but is a level of spiritual attainment which all mankind will reach and which many already have attained.

karma: that which befalls an individual because of prior thoughts and deeds, in this or former lifetimes. Can be good or bad, positive or negative.

karma, law of: otherwise known as law of cause and effect. What one sows, so shall he reap.

Karmic Board: that department of the spiritual Hierarchy which reviews and passes on each individual's soul or akashic record. Assigns or permits incarnations, lessons, roles, missions for everyone in this solar system.

karmic debt: that which one owes payment for, due to action in this or prior lifetimes. Must be paid off at some time in a spiritually proper manner.

kingdoms: celestial, man, animal, vegetable, mineral, devic. Denotes a category of divine creation. Evolution is only within the same kingdom, never through the various kingdoms. Transmigration–incarnation of an entity in different kingdoms–is an invalid theory.

language, universal sign: transmission of messages, commands, energies or stories through higher plane control of body movements, especially arms and hands, of a channel.

Lemuria: civilization dating from 26,000,000 to 10,000 years ago. Land area was from western USA out into Pacific Ocean. Final destruction was 10,000–13,000 years ago; allegory of Noah and the Flood.

levitation: lifting one's body off the ground by spiritual or by higher plane equipment means.

light: spiritual illumination; spiritual; etheric. Also, God as Light.

light body: fourth dimensional body of man; his etheric or Christ body; one of the seven bodies relating to Earth living; the resurrected or ascended body through which the Christ powers and talents can be demonstrated.

light worker: a spiritual worker in the hierarchal plan and program.

Lord: God; laws of God; spiritual title for officeholder in Hierarchy; designation given to one who has mastered all laws of a specified realm.

Love God and Love One Another: the two laws which Christ Jesus gave unto man of Earth. The motto of the White Brotherhood, the light workers in this solar system.

Love In Action: the New Age teaching of action with high Self, action with love; the Mark-Age theme and motto.

Mark Age: designation of the Latter-Day period (1960–2000), when there are appearing signs of the times to demonstrate the ending of the old age. Also, designation for the Earth plane aspect of that hierarchal plan. Also, the spiritual name for El Morya in his incarnation on Earth as Charles Boyd Gentzel (1922–1981), cofounder of Mark-Age Unit.

Mark-Age: with the hyphen, designates the unit cofounded in 1960 by incarnated Hierarchal Board members El Morya (Charles Boyd Gentzel) and Nada (Yolanda of the Sun, or Pauline Sharpe). One of many focal points on Earth for the Hierarchal Board. Coordination Unit #7 and initial focus for externalization of the Hierarchal Board on Earth in the Latter Days.

master: one who has mastered something. An ascended master is one who has achieved Christhood and has translated or has raised his or her physical body to the fourth dimension.

master ship #10: mother-ship spacecraft of city size which is Sananda's headquarters for the Second Coming program. Has been in etheric orbit around Earth since about 1885. Will be seen by those on Earth when

157

time approaches for Sananda's return to Earth as Christ Jesus of Nazareth and as Sananda, Prince of Earth. Also known as Star of Bethlehem.

materialization: coupled with dematerialization. Mat and demat are a transmutation or translation from one frequency vibration to another, from one plane or realm to another. Translation of chemical, electronic and auric fields of an individual or object.

meditation: spiritual contemplation to receive illumination, or to experience at-onement with Spirit or one's own Christ Self or another agent of Spirit, or to pray or to decree or to visualize desired results.

mental body: one of the seven bodies of man pertaining to Earth living. Does not look like a physical body.

metaphysics: spiritual meaning is the study of that which lies beyond the physical, of the basic spiritual laws of the universe, and the practical application thereof in daily life on Earth.

miracle: a spiritual manifestation, or a work. There are no so-called miracles possible, in the sense of circumventing a divine law.

mortal consciousness: the awareness of a soul during Earth incarnation, prior to Christ consciousness.

negative polarity: refers to the female principle in creation. The rest or passive nature, as complementing the positive or action polarity.

New Age: the incoming Golden Age or Aquarian Age. Actually began entry about 1960.

Om; or Aum: a designation for God. Means power.

one hundred and forty-four thousand: the elect, the demonstrators and the teachers of Christ powers during the Latter Days. The number is literal, in that at least that number must so demonstrate to achieve the spiritual goal of lifting man into the fourth dimension, and symbolic, in that it does not preclude any number of additional ones from being included.

physical body: one of the seven bodies of man for living on Earth. Has been expressing in the third dimension, but is evolving into the fourth dimension. The vehicle for mortal expression of the soul on Earth. The physical on other planets of our solar system expresses as high as the eighth dimension.

plane: a realm, a dimension, a level of expression.

positive polarity: the male or action focus, as complementing the negative or female or passive polarity.

prince: a spiritual office and title, such as Sananda being Prince of Love and Peace as Chohan of Seventh Ray, and Prince of Earth as spiritual ruler of this planet.

prophet: in addition to usual meaning it is the term preferred by those of higher planes in referring to a communications channel.

psychic: refers to the powers of man focused through the solar plexus chakra or center. Not as high as the Christ powers.

realm: plane, dimension, a level of expression.

reincarnation: taking on another incarnation, on any plane or planet, during one's eternal life.

Sananda: Chohan of Seventh Ray. Prince or spiritual ruler of Earth. One of Council of Seven, highest ruling body of the solar system. Previous Earth incarnations: Christ Jesus of Nazareth, his last one; biblical Melchizedek, Moses and Elijah; Zarathustra; Gautama Buddha; Socrates, Greek philosopher; leader of Abels, in allegorical story of Cain and Abel; leader of Noahs, in allegorical story of Noah and the ark. Presently located in etheric realm, from whence he directs entire operation for upliftment of man and his own Second Coming; headquarters is master ship #10, in etheric orbit around Earth since about 1885.

Saturnian Council: Council of Seven, highest ruling body of the solar system. Headquarters is on planet Saturn.

Second Coming: refers to each coming into awareness of his or her own Christ Self, and the return of Sananda as Jesus of Nazareth to institute spiritual government on Earth early in the twenty-first century.

Self, high: Christ Self, I Am presence, superconscious, oversoul, Atman, Yahweh (Jehovah). The spiritual Self of each individual. Differentiated, in writing, from mortal self by use of capital *S* in Self.

self, mortal: the spiritually unawakened consciousness of Earthman.

sensitive: a channel, prophet, instrument, medium. One who is sensitive to or aware of spiritual realms and occupants therein.

Seven Rays of Life: the seven major groupings of aspects of God; the Seven Flames. First: will and power (blue). Second: intelligence and wisdom (yellow). Third: personal love and feeling (pink). Fourth: crystallization (colorless, crystal clear). Fifth: unity, integration, healing, balance (green). Sixth: transmutation, cleansing, purification (violet). Seventh: divine love, peace, rest (gold and white). As channeled numerous times by Yolanda.

Son of God: with capital *S* for Son, denotes the Christ body of all mankind, collectively. With small *s* for son, denotes an individual. All men are sons of God and eventually will come into that awareness, heritage, power and cocreativity with God.

Son, only begotten: refers to the entire Christ body, which includes all of mankind, and not just a single individual.

soul: the accumulation of an individual's experiences in his or her eternal living. A covering or a coat of protection, over which the individual spirit can and does rely for its manifestations.

soul mate: one with whom an individual has had close and favorable association in one or more lifetimes. Each person thus has had many soul mates, but does not incarnate with or come into contact with all of them during any one lifetime.

soul, twin: as an individual soul develops, it expresses in male and female embodiments. Eventually it will begin to gravitate toward either male or female for its expression in the Christ realms. While so developing, Spirit guides another soul toward the opposite polarity along the same path. Thus when one enters the Christ realm as a male polarity, there will be one of female polarity to complement and to supplement, with the same general background and abilities. Thus each person has a twin soul. But this term does not mean one soul was split, to gain experiences, and then eventually merges back into oneness. Twin souls are two separate individualities at all times.

sphere: planet, realm, plane, dimension, level of expression.

Spirit: God, Creative Energy, Creative Force, Divine Mind, Father-Mother God, Original Source.

spirit: the spiritual consciousness or Self of man.

spiritual: term preferred over *religious* when referring to spiritual matters, as there are specific dogma and connotation attached to *religious.*

subconscious: one of the three phases of mind. Denotes the soul or record-keeper phase, which also performs the automatic and maintenance functions of the physical body. The relay phase between the superconscious and conscious aspects of one's total consciousness.

superconscious: the highest of the three aspects of individual consciousness, consisting also of conscious and subconscious aspects. The Christ, I Am, real, high Self. The real individual, which projects into embodiment via having created a physical body for such incarnation.

sword of truth: denotes the use of God's word and law to eliminate error, and to guide and to protect spiritual persons.

teacher, spiritual: one who teaches spiritual matters. May be on this or a higher plane.

teleportation: spiritual power enabling one to move from one location to another via dematerialization and materialization, without physical means. A Christ power. Symbol for this in Atlantis was dodo bird.

tests, spiritual: tests of one's spiritual progress and lessons learned, given by Spirit, by one's own Christ Self or by other spiritual teachers. Not temptings, which never are given anyone by any of the above guides.

third dimension: the frequency vibrational level in which Earth and all on it have been expressing physically for eons. Being transmuted into the fourth dimension, which was begun gradually by the mid-twentieth century for completion in the twenty-first century, but well into the process by the end of the twentieth. Does not refer to the three dimensions of length, width and height, but to a range of vibration.

thought form: an actual form beyond the third dimension, created by man's thoughts. Has substance in another plane and can take on limited powers and activities, based on the power man has instilled in it through his thoughts and beliefs.

thought temperature: the attitudes of an individual or a group concerning a certain topic.

transfiguration: a change of one's features, or of entire body, caused by overshadowing by one's Christ Self or by an ascended master.

transition: term denoting death of an individual on one plane so as to begin a new life on another plane. Also, general meaning of making a change.

transmutation: spiritually, refers to purifying one's mortal consciousness and body so as to permit raising into fourth dimension, physically and as concerns Christ consciousness.

trials: spiritual tests given one in evolution to see if lessons are learned or if obstacles can be overcome, as in training for a soul mission.

Trinity, Holy: Father-Mother-Son, Father-Holy Spirit-Son, Father-Holy Ghost-Son. The three aspects of God.

twenty-six-million-year cycle: a period of evolution for man in this solar system. The cycle since the final fall of man on Earth, during which the Elder race has been attempting to raise the human race that had become entrapped in the third dimension. Cycle ended about A.D. 2000.

twenty-six-thousand-year cycle: the period of time, since the beginning of the fall of Atlantis, in which man of Earth has been given the last opportunity in this solar system for reevolution into the fourth dimension. Duration of a hierarchal plan and program to raise man from the third dimension into true status as sons of God. Cycle ended about A.D. 2000.

two-hundred-and-six-million-year cycle: an evolutionary cycle for man involving graduation in and around the central sun from which we originated. The period during which man has experimented with life form on Earth in the third dimension. Cycle ended about A.D. 2000.

two-hundred-and-six-thousand-year cycle: withdrawal of Elder race from on Earth; decline of Lemuria. Cycle ended about A.D. 2000.

veil, seventh: final veil separating man from knowing his divine heritage and powers.

vibrations: the frequency range in which something is expressing; not in terms of cycles per second, or any present Earth understanding and terminology. Also, the radiations emitted by an individual, able to be received consciously by one spiritually sensitive to such emanations.

world, end of: denotes ending of third dimensional expression for Earth and all on it, physically, and entry into a higher level of frequency vibration, the fourth dimension. The end of the materially-minded world of man so as to begin spiritual understanding and evolvement. Does not mean end of the Earth, but only entering a higher dimension.

Mark-Age Mastership Books

HOW TO DO ALL THINGS. Your use of divine power. Achieve union with your inner Self. Demonstrate your true heritage, nature & powers as a child of God. By El Morya/Mark. **$8**

FACTS OF LIFE. Unparalleled guidebook on meditation, love, karma & reincarnation, channeling, discernment, UFOs, Second Coming, sex, more. By Nada-Yolanda. **$15**

BIRTH OF THE LIGHT BODY. Master twelve spiritual qualities of your I Am Self, as symbolized by twelve apostles of Christ Jesus. By Nada-Yolanda, with Robert H. Knapp, M.D. **$17**

PROPHECIES: 2000–4000 A.D. Ascended masters reveal critical guidelines for the next two thousand years. Prepare for Second Coming. Channeled via Nada-Yolanda. **$10**

METAMORPHOSIS. Ascended masters describe fascinating mortal transformation, or *metamorphosis,* into light body of immortal, I Am Self. Channeled via Nada-Yolanda. **$15**

CONTACTS FROM THE FOURTH DIMENSION. Battle of Armageddon, judgment day. Titanic conflict between forces of light & darkness. Channeled via Nada-Yolanda. **$20**

EVOLUTION OF MAN. Origin, history, destiny of man. Nature & powers of I Am consciousness. Major evolutionary cycles. Lemuria & Atlantis. Channeled via Nada-Yolanda. **$15**

ANGELS & MAN. Seven archangels reveal nature & function of angels, unveiling cosmic relationship with & guardianship of man. Channeled via Nada-Yolanda. **$15**

1000 KEYS TO THE TRUTH. Guidelines for Latter Days, Second Coming, karma, reincarnation, ascended masters, light body, more. Based on channelings of Nada-Yolanda. **$7**

MAPP* TO AQUARIUS: *Mark Age Period & Program. Navigate the New Age with a tested road map for the Latter Days. Channeled via Nada-Yolanda. **$15**

VISITORS FROM OTHER PLANETS. Who they are & why they are here to assist our evolution into the New Age. Federation of Planets. Landings. Channeled via Nada-Yolanda. **$15**

LIFE IN OUR SOLAR SYSTEM. Extraordinary afterlife experiences of Gloria Lee. Adventures in higher realms. Life on other planes & planets. Channeled via Nada-Yolanda. **$16**

Mark-Age • P.O. Box 10 • Pioneer, TN 37847, USA